The Journey To Forgiveness

Releasing Hurtful Feelings

and Moving On

DR BRUCE S. RILEY, LMFT

DEDICATION

I want to dedicate this book to my rock, Karen Z. Riley. This wonderful lady has far exceeded my expectations as a wife, mother, and true friend. She has helped me in ways that are unimaginable. I am forever indebted to this woman of God who prays for me often and allows me time to pursue writings like this.

CONTENTS

ACKNOWLEDGMENTS

I am so appreciative to Andrea Sanders, Alesia Cooper, Davonna Austin-Brazil, Janae Burns, Janelle Burns, Lucy Merriweather, Carla Richards, Tanosha Tucker-Johnson, Karen Riley, Alycia Jones, Donna Jones, and LaShawn Saiz for their editorial assistance. May God bless them for extending to me such a great labor of love. I am truly grateful.

CHAPTER 1

FORGIVENESS IS A PLACE

Forgiveness is place. It's a place in your soul that allows you to be at rest; where you no longer allow the torment of someone else's behavior towards you to be a source of pain and discomfort. It's an emotional place of calm where you have resolved to be rid of thoughts and feelings that cause stress, anger, depression, or any other destructive impulses.

It takes a little while to get there. Anyone can go, but not everyone does. Why not? To get to the place of forgiveness a choice must be made. But not everyone chooses. Our choices are a matter of the will. Not everyone wants to forgive. Some would rather cherish the thought of sweet revenge, or to comfort themselves in self-pity. Our sense of justice and fair play can sometimes immobilize us to go no further until we are vindicated by God or that the offenders know that they didn't get away with it.

The place of forgiveness is the place where you learn to heal from the hurts, disappointments, and frustrations inflicted upon you by others whether they meant it or not.

Getting to the place of forgiveness means that you learn to do something with the hurt that seems like it will never go away. You will learn that you are more powerful than the pain inflicted upon you, and that you can survive what you thought might kill you.

I had to go to that place of forgiveness when it came to a woman that I needed to forgive. This elderly woman was a weekly torment in my life. Being a part of the church where I was pastor caused me to see her at least once a week. She constantly made condescending remarks to other young Christians and annoyed me with comments about how she felt about things in the church. She basically had something negative to say about everything all the time.

Things got so bad in how she affected me that I began to hate her. One day I saw her coming across the streets towards the church and I somehow wished that a truck would come along and put her out of my misery. Yes, my misery. Thankfully, the truck did not answer my prayer.

She was not that open to correction, and yet I did not want to put her out of the church. When I saw her my stomach would begin to churn. Later, I began to seek the Lord about this matter and the Lord instructed me to forgive her. I would say, "Lord, I forgive _____". The churning continued. I would say the next day, "Lord, I forgive _____". The churning continued. I would pray this prayer to forgive her every day for what seemed about six weeks. Then, one Sunday I saw her, and the churning had stopped. I no longer felt the hatred towards her. I had forgiven her. What a great relief. She no longer affected me the same way anymore. Now I could love her.

Sometime later, after she eventually left the church, I got word that she had been stricken with cancer. No, I was not glad to hear that. My heart had become more compassionate. I was asked to go to the hospital to pray for her. Perhaps in times past, when I was under the control of my own bitterness, I might have refused to go to the hospital. But I went with the intention of demonstrating my love for her. Miraculously, God worked a miracle and she was healed of the cancer. It was a glorious display of the grace and mercy of almighty God. But to my dismay something unusual occurred…she never changed. I realized that the forgiveness was for me, not her. I had changed. God helped me to see how marvelous his mercy was to me. I could have gotten the cancer, but instead he helped me see the healing power of his forgiveness for which I am grateful.

Forgiveness is a place of Healing and Restoration. Many times, when forgiveness is achieved, marriages that were headed towards divorce are healed; friends are talking again; debts are forgiven and not brought up again; and even next-door neighbors can talk over the fence once again.

It happened in a one-room Amish school in Nickel Mines, Pennsylvania on Monday morning, October2, 2006. A demonic thirty-two-year-old Charles Roberts entered the school with an automatic rifle and four hundred rounds of ammunition. He told the 15 boys and the teacher to leave the classroom while he tied up the ten girls who remained. A brave thirteen-year-old, the oldest of the hostages, pleaded with Roberts to "Shoot me first and let the little ones go." But instead, Roberts shot all of them, killing five and leaving the other five severely wounded. When the police stormed the building, Roberts then shot himself. Before opening fire on the children, he told them "I'm angry at God for taking my little daughter".

This unthinkable massacre spread across the United States and around the world. There were over fifty television news crews in Nickel Mines the next day, taking pictures, interviewing survivors, parents, and school officials until the killer and those who died were buried. Shortly thereafter, the story captured the hearts of America when it was learned that the Amish parents began to share words of forgiveness towards the family of the killer, Charles Roberts.

People who heard the story could hardly believe that forgiveness could be granted so soon after the vicious and senseless killing by parents who lost their precious children in such a horrific way. The news reports of this act of forgiveness became the focal point in many papers, the internet, and television news stories. In fact, one week after the murders, Amish forgiveness was the main topic in more than

2,400 news stories around the world. The New York Times, USA Today, The Washington Post, Newsweek, NBC Nightly News, CBS Morning News, Larry King Live, Fox News, Oprah, and dozens of other media outlets praised the forgiving Amish. Three weeks later, "Amish forgiveness" had appeared in 2,900 news stories around the world and on 534,000 web sites.

Many people believed that what the Amish did in forgiving the killer came too soon, and that it was hasty and mentally unhealthy. A grandmother laughed when I asked if the forgiveness was orchestrated. "You mean that some people actually thought we had a meeting to plan forgiveness?"

One father of one slain daughter said, "Our forgiveness

was not our words, it was what we did." A great number of those in the Amish community visited the killer's widow bringing food and flowers and hugged the members of his family. The thing that communicated Amish forgiveness was the words of encouragement, hugs, gifts, and their mere presence. They call this "Acts of Grace". There were

75 people at the killer's burial. Half of the people there were Amish, which included some of the parents who had just buried their own children. They also contributed money to the killer's family support fund.

For most people, the act of forgiveness doesn't come until after a long emotional journey – sometimes years, and for some never. The Amish make the journey very short. Their religious tenant encourages them to forgive even before injustice occurs.

Amish faith is grounded in the teachings of Jesus to love enemies, reject revenge, and leave vengeance in the hands of God. As a father who lost a daughter in the schoolhouse said, "Forgiveness means giving up the right to revenge." The Amish believe that God's arm of justice removes the need for human retaliation or going through lawyers to protect their rights here.

The Amish believe that not only "If we don't forgive, we won't be forgiven", but that their salvation hinges on the willingness to forgive, which is a powerful motivation to extend. One Bishop, while discussing the Lord's Prayer, stated that "Forgiveness is the only thing that Jesus underscored in the Lord's Prayer."

While forgiveness means not holding a grudge – "the acid

of bitterness eats the container that holds it," one farmer explained – the Amish are clear that it does not free the offender from punishment. Had the gunman survived, they would have wanted him locked up, not for revenge but to protect other children.

Although there were no expressions of outright rage or hopes that the gunman would burn in hell, the wanton slaughter of their children did bring deep pain, tears, and raw grief. The Amish still find forgiveness to be an emotional journey, but their act of grace was the beginning of their healing.

It is unfortunate that many Christians look at forgiveness as optional; that it is something that you do if you can. If we take the approach of the Amish and display it as soon as the offense takes place, it will speed up the journey, and allow the process to gain some momentum.

If you are a Christian, do not take this grace of forgiveness for granted. God gave it to us to make our lives better and as a witness to those who don't know him. So, look at it this way, forgiveness is a place where you allow divine intervention to operate for you in ways that only Jesus can.

> "Forgiveness doesn't excuse their actions. Forgiveness stops their actions from destroying yours."

Unknown

CHAPTER 2

BEGINNING THE JOURNEY

Beginning this Journey to Forgiveness requires one thing…a decision. You may not even feel like it, but I urge you to start. To not decide is to leave yourself stuck with the possibility that the way you currently feel may not get any better.

Once you move towards forgiveness the process of healing begins. To begin this journey is allowing yourself to look outside of yourself; it's looking towards others; it's seeing that your concern for the welfare of others removes you from the 'pity party' and gives you a strength that you may be thinking you could never have.

You might be feeling miserable right now, wondering if you will ever feel like loving another human being as long as you live. You might be thinking that no one is even worthy to receive your love or friendship again. You might have vengeance on your mind and could be contemplating how to put your plan into action. Now you may have already realized that your 'Game of Thrones' retaliation move might cause you to get arrested and live out your days in prison may not be the best remedy for the hurt and pain that you feel.

What if you forgive and can feel whole again? What if you move towards forgiveness and the offender (or the person who you believe offended you) can be won back to you? What if you realize that the relationship is more valuable than to just let it end? You see, there are some amazing possibilities for a better future if forgiveness is given a chance. How about it?

Are you ready to start this journey? If you are, then say this, "I have the power to forgive. And with the help of God, I will."

As was said, this journey requires a decision. If you choose to take this journey, know it is not a 'Mission Impossible", but rather a challenge to rescue yourself from a life of holding grudges to feeling free, and open for love to just flood your heart. You are being led by the Spirit of God to do what he is helping you to do – forgive.

Isaiah 41:10 (NIV)
"So do not fear, for I am with you; do not be dismayed, for I am your God. I will strengthen you and help you; I will uphold you with my righteous right hand."

Here's what you can take on your journey:

1. The Bible – Eat regularly
2. Prayer – Breath the breath of God
3. Confession of Sin – Spiritual cleansing

4. Fellowship – Association with a caring group of believers
5. Worship – Spiritual exercise
6. Self -Denial – Strength to take initiative

1. **The Bible**

By consuming the Word of God daily, you will be strong enough to resist the desire to hold on to old behaviors that resist forgiveness. The Word of God teaches you not to hold on to grudges, or to refuse to forgive those who hurt you.

By taking the Word of God with you, you will not only know the will of God about forgiveness, but you will increase your desire to share loving kindness. The Word of God conditions your heart to love like God loves.

<u>Colossians 3:12-14</u> (ESV)
"Put on then, as God's chosen ones, holy and beloved, compassionate hearts, kindness, humility, meekness, and patience, bearing with one another and, if one has a complaint against another, forgiving each other; as the Lord has forgiven you, so you also must forgive. And above all these put on love, which binds everything together in perfect harmony."

<u>John 6:51</u> (NIV)
"I am the living bread that came down from heaven. Whoever eats this bread will live forever. This bread is my flesh, which I will give for the life of the world."

2. **Prayer**

One of the priorities of moving along this journey is to talk to the Lord about the situations and conditions in which you find yourself needing to ask his help. The Lord is in readiness to help you unload the suitcases of anger or hatred that have been packed to go with you. Of course, if these bags go with you, you will be overloaded and slowed down from reaching forgiveness.

It's easy to forgive those you pray for. If you don't pray for the people who hurt or betray you, it's very easy for the root of bitterness to imbed itself deeper into your heart and build up a stronghold of hatred that will forbid any consideration to forgive.

<u>James 5:16</u> (NIV)

"Therefore, confess your sins to each other and pray for each other so that you may be healed. The prayer of a righteous person is powerful and effective."

3. **Confession of Sin**

As you journey, getting closer to God as you go, you may realize that the attitudes that foster and comfort resentment are really sinful tendencies that are inconsistent for a growing Christian. The holiness of God will object to what you try to hold onto when you come into His presence. Even if you try to justify why you hold this person in contempt, the Spirit of God won't allow it. Remember this: Another person's sinful behavior never justifies the same measure of rejection.

Even as I write this book, my heart is searching my emotional data base for people I have put on my "list" of people that I absolutely want nothing to do with. I realize that I need to go back and revisit how I really feel about them and the need to confess the bad feelings that I have towards them and ask the Lord to forgive me for not loving them the way I should.

1 John 1:9 (KJV)
"If we confess our sins, he is faithful and just to forgive us [our] sins, and to cleanse us from all unrighteousness."

4. Fellowship

Being in the company of other supportive Christians will certainly cause you to know that you are loved despite unfortunate relationship issues with others. These individuals are placed in your life to help give you perspective on how you might be handling this matter of forgiving others.

Good fellowship will allow you to enrich your capacity to love others and build your ability to forgive others. I would like you to look at forgiveness as a withdrawal from your "Love Account" that you have accumulated from healthy relationships and loving fellowship that God has given you. Take the time and begin to thank God for all the wonderful people He has put in your life.

Now if your circle of fellowship is small, it might indicate that you might have limited yourself perhaps with a spirit of fear that makes you afraid of making more than a few friends. If it's been at least a year since you've added some new friends, then it's time to reach beyond your comfort zone and extend yourself into other people's lives. Build up your fellowship so that you will be so strong in love that forgiving other people will become a regular part of your Christian discipline.

Ephesians 4:2-3 (NIV)
"²Be completely humble and gentle; be patient, bearing with one another in love. ³Make every effort to keep the unity of the Spirit through the bond of peace."

5. Worship

Being in the House of God, and coming into the presence of God, creates opportunities for the Spirit of God to impart influence upon you to engage with the will and heart of God. As you worship, surrender your wants and needs to God, and allow him to edit your life for His glory.

Bless Him for everything He has already done, knowing that He has been so good to you that you dare not leave his presence with anger or hatred in your heart. Worship is total obedience to God. While you are engaged in worship, ask God what he wants you to do concerning the person you need to forgive.

Hebrews 10:24-25 (ESV) *"²⁴And let us consider how to stir up one another to love and good works, ²⁵ not neglecting to meet together, as is the habit of some, but encouraging one another, and all the more as you see the Day drawing near."*

6. Self-Denial

You are a part of a community. The notion of self-denial is to make sacrifices that remedy situations for the betterment of the whole. There have been so many families that have been severely hampered by grudges between family members and then passed down through siblings and other relatives for so long, that nobody knows what the original feud was about.

Your maturity and level of love will grow when you take the initiative to talk to someone you have an issue with or bring people together to resolve issues that threaten togetherness and the performance of the will of God. By doing this you also develop humility and foster greater fellowship among others.

Every day is an opportunity to reflect God on the life of someone who may not know Christ as well. You have been chosen to help reconcile others to Christ. This is to be recognized in the relationships that have been strained or in cases in which you have been wounded.

<u>**Isaiah 1:18**</u> (NIV)
"Come now, let us settle the matter," says the LORD. "Though your sins are like scarlet, they shall be as white as snow; though they are red as crimson, they shall be like wool."

<u>**Matthew 5:23-24**</u> (NIV)
"23Therefore, if you are offering your gift at the altar and there remember that your brother or sister has something against
you, 24 leave your gift there in front of the altar. First go and be reconciled to them; then come and offer your gift."

As you embark on this journey, know that God is with you, and wants you to know the forgiveness that you render is an act of mercy and that you are a vessel in the hand of God.

> "Forgiveness is not granted because a person deserves to be forgiven. No one deserves to be forgiven. Forgiveness is a deliberate act of love, mercy, and grace. Forgiveness is a decision to not hold something against another person, despite what he or she has done to you."
>
> www. Gotquestions.org/what-is-forgivneness.html

CHAPTER 3

THE DISEASE OF UNFORGIVENESS

The feelings that come upon you when someone harms you physically or emotionally can be very intense, such as sadness, anger, or resentment. It is possible to dwell so much on what was done wrong to you that you can begin to feel extreme hatred towards that person. It's even worse when the person who hurts you feels no need to apologize. You may also want revenge.

Anytime you hold an ill-will or resentment against someone for a wrong that they have committed against you is called a 'grudge'. Anytime you do not readily forgive someone who wrongs you, you are holding a grudge. I submit to you that there are negative consequences, even health problems associated with holding a grudge.

A study by the Social Psychiatry and Psychiatric Epidemiology Journal in 2010 asked nearly 10,000 U.S.

residents if they held grudges against other people for years. The Journal reported that more than 6,500 people responded. The researchers Erick Messias, Anil Saini, Phillip Sinato, and Stephen Welch reported that those persons, who said they held grudges, reported they experienced higher rates of heart disease and cardiac arrest, elevated blood pressure, stomach ulcers, arthritis, back problems, headaches, and chronic pain than those who did not hold grudges. While much more study was requested on this matter, there seems to be an obvious link between unforgiveness and health problems.

There may also be a link between practicing forgiveness and health benefits. A survey given in 2003 published in the Journal for the Scientific Study of Religion, in which 1,500 Christian older adults (age 66 and older) in the U.S. revealed that those who generally practiced forgiveness reported greater personal well-being, including lower levels of depression and physical health complaints as well as greater levels of life satisfaction.

Unforgiveness is classified in medical books as a disease. According to Dr. Steven Standiford, chief of surgery at the Cancer Treatment Centers of America, refusing to forgive makes people sick and keeps them that way. With that in mind, forgiveness therapy is now being used to help treat diseases, such as cancer. "It's important to treat emotional wounds or disorders because they really can hinder someone's reactions to the treatments, even someone's willingness to pursue treatment," Standiford explained.

Of all cancer patients, 61 percent have forgiveness issues, and of those, more than half are severe, according to research by Dr. Michael Barry, a pastor and the author of the book, The Forgiveness Project. "Harboring these negative emotions, this anger and hatred, creates a state of chronic anxiety," he said.

In short, holding a grudge can make you sick. We are a three-fold being of body, soul, and spirit. Our body may be well, and we may recognize our fellowship with God as our creator and the object of our worship, but when we allow the dis-ease (to be removed from ease) of anger, hatred, resentment, and an unwillingness to forgive to stay in our heart, it creates a schism, or a division in us that affects the body's health in a negative way. This is the sickness.

Here is an example of (the) kind of forgiveness that comes forth from a heart that feels compassion and concern for the welfare of those who have erred in their lives and yet can be spared a most difficult life:

Matthew   18:21-27 (NRSV)

"21 Then Peter came and said to him, "Lord, if another member of the church sins against me, how often should I forgive? As many as seven times?"

22Jesus said to him, "Not seven times, but I tell you, seventy-seven times.

23"For this reason the kingdom of heaven may be compared to a king who wished to settle accounts with his slaves. 24When he began the reckoning, one who owed him ten thousand talents was brought to him; 25 and, as he could not pay, his lord ordered him to be sold, together with his wife and children and all his possessions, and payment to be made. 26So the slave fell on his knees before him, saying, 'Have patience with me, and I will pay you everything.' 27And out of pity for him, the lord of that slave released him and forgave him the debt."

The reason we must extend forgiveness indefinitely is so we can be prepared to defend ourselves from giving permission for the grudge or retaliation to have access to the way we deal with the person who harms us. It seems that the Lord knows that we have the tendency to give people the "Three Strikes and You're Out" treatment. The Lord wants us to extend our patience with others not until we've had enough, but until they've had enough, and begin to change their life appropriately because of our mercy.

You see, the Lord wants the change to take place in us first, and then in the wrongdoer. Real forgiveness will be absent when we don't first take the focus on what we have lost and see the misfortune upon the other person. This man in the scripture above was in jeopardy of not only losing his possessions but his wife and children. This man had the potential of turning his life around. If you read on further, you will see that he blew his chance for a better life. So, as far as you and I are concerned, we are not to be concerned with what a person does with the mercy extended to them, we have to allow the Lord to make us better so the actions of others does not make us sick.

When you forgive, you in
no way change the past –
but you sure do change
the future

Bernard Meltzer

CHAPTER 4

PAST THE HARBOR

Some can forgive a lot sooner than others. Perhaps it might be important to check to see if you might be carrying some dangerous cargo or be weighed down with thoughts or behaviors that may put the entire journey in jeopardy.

According to Wikipedia, A harbor is a sheltered body of water where ships, boats, and barges can be docked. The term harbor is often used interchangeably with port, which is a man-made facility built for loading and unloading vessels and dropping off and picking up passengers. But it can also refer to the keeping of thoughts or feelings in one's mind, especially secretly.

On this journey to forgiveness, it is vitally important to drop off that which may hinder the journey and may even cause permanent damage to the mind or body. If you don't forgive, what happens? Too often, a person may say they forgive; that it is the Christian thing to do, but they may not have forgiven. You may still be harboring unforgiveness and not know it.

Ephesians 4:31(NIV) *"Get rid of all bitterness, rage and anger, brawling and slander, along with every form of malice."*

Don't forget that you want to prevent the impact of these negative emotions in your body and spirit. How do you avoid letting these emotions take control in your life?

It might help to remind yourself what could happen if negative emotions can remain. Consider the type of person you could become if you replace them with the right emotions. Jesus said, *"Father, forgive them, for they know not what they do* (Luke 23:34). Focus on what could happen to them as the forgiveness of God is applied to their life. Forgiven people tend to be more grateful. I know I am.

I choose CONTENTMENT over BITTERNESS.
"I'm satisfied with my life, and I turn it over to Jesus"

I choose CALM over RAGE.
"I'm waiting patiently on the Lord"

I choose TOLERANCE over ANGER.
"I will not let the behavior or words from others move me"

I choose AGREEMENT over BRAWLING
"I will seek to be in harmony with those in my life"

I choose COMPLIMENTS over SLANDER
"I will speak well of everyone I know"

I choose FRIENDLINESS over MALICE
"I will treat everyone I know with kindness"

Hebrews 12:1 (NIV)

"Therefore, since we are surrounded by such a great cloud of witnesses, let us throw off everything that hinders and the sin that so easily entangles. And let us run with perseverance the race marked out for us,"

It's beneficial to follow the examples of those patriarchs that have gone before us and trusted God through the most severe conditions. Don't forget that God has a purpose for your life. Satan wants you to be distracted by the intentional or unintentional hurts inflicted on you by others. The sooner you can resolve these obstacles, the sooner you can attend to the plans God has for your life.

Bill Barnes, in his book, "The Songs of Deliverance", talks about three natural steps necessary for true forgiveness:
Step 1.   Confess the unforgiveness, bitterness, or hatred as sin, because that is how God views it.

Step 2.   Renounce the unforgiveness, bitterness, or hatred. Make the decision to break away fully from the unforgiveness. We must make the decision not to walk in agreement with Satan or any of his works, or any other works of darkness – to sever ourselves from any ties with him. Thus, we must fall out of agreement with the unforgiveness.

Step 3.   Make the decision in your mind, and confess it

with your mouth, to forgive that person, or persons who have hurt or wronged you. Forgive them each by name, individually and specifically and ask the Lord to forgive them.

Dead Man Walking

"I paid little attention as the glare of headlights briefly illuminated my boyfriend Mark's face and then swept on…" So begins Debbie Morris's amazing story of suffering and forgiveness. On a Friday night in the 1980's Debbie and her boyfriend Mark were kidnapped while on a date. One of the kidnappers was Robert Willie, the character made famous in the Susan Sarandon, Sean Penn movie Dead Man Walking. After shooting her boyfriend in the head and leaving him for dead in the woods, the kidnappers subjected Debbie to two terrifying days of rape and brutalization.

Just two days in a lifetime, yet they understandably left an indelible Mark on Debbie's life. She spent years struggling with pain, anger, depression, alcohol abuse and guilt. Most remarkable of all, however, is her journey towards healing and forgiveness.

In the book 'Forgiving the Dead Man Walking' she tells how she learned to forgive her kidnappers. She realized that she needed to forgive Willie, if nothing better, for her own good. She had seen the way rage and bitterness consumed the lives of the parents of another girl raped and murdered by her kidnappers. She didn't want to become a prisoner of her past. And so, the night Robert Willie was executed, Debbie realized she could forgive him. She prayed, "Lord, I really do need to forgive Robert Willie. As best I can anyway. If the execution goes on, make it fast and painless. I don't want him to suffer anymore."

But what does it mean to forgive in a situation like this? Debbie describes how helpful psychology professor Dr. Terry Hargrave was. Dr. Hargraves divides forgiveness into two parts: salvage and restoration. Salvage involves insight – recognizing how we were violated and who bears responsibility and understanding – trying to understand why something was done. Restoration involves overt forgiving, where forgiveness is openly sought, given and received and compensation, where there are things which compensate us for past hurts. Hargraves explains that restoration is possible only where there was a prior relationship, or a relationship you want to restore. This was not the case with Debbie. For her salvage was the highest goal she could seek. With its twin dimensions of insight and understanding, it's allowed her to move beyond herself blame and bitterness to "salvage" something from her hurtful experience.

Debbie was also helped by Lewis book Forgive and Forget. In a section "forgiving Monsters" Smedes writes "If monsters are beyond forgiving, we give them a power they should never have…The climax of forgiveness takes two, I know. But you can have the reality of forgiveness without its climax. Forgiving is real, even if it stops at the healing of the forgiver" In this light, Debbie writes "The refusal to forgive him meant that I held onto all my Robert Willie-related stuff – my pain, my shame, my self-pity. That's what I gave up in forgiving him. And it wasn't until I did, that real healing could even begin. I was the one who gained."

Throughout this process, Debbie has struggled with what she feels about the death penalty. She closes her book with these words, "God seems to put a higher priority on forgiveness than on justice. We don't sing 'Amazing Justice', we sing 'Amazing Grace'. Does that mean I think a holy God would oppose the execution of a convicted murderer like Robert Willie? I don't know; I'm still wrestling with that question. But I do know this: Justice didn't do a thing to heal me. Forgiveness did."

Source: Based on reports in Debbie Morris, Forgiving the Dead Man Walking (Zondervan, 1998)

Holding anger is a poison. It eats you from the inside. We think that hatred is the weapon that attacks the person who harmed us. But hatred is a curved blade. And the harm we do, we do to ourselves.

- 5 people you meet in heaven

CHAPTER 5

THE VALLEY OF DEPRESSION

In the mornings, Valerie had been leaving for work before Victor, who was just getting up when the Uber driver would be coming to pick her up. Jamie, her daughter, was picked up by her two friends to go to the local high school 45 minutes after mom left. Before she left, Victor had told Valerie that he was missing their usual moments of intimacy a few times during the week. Valerie insisted that they would begin again once their before-work staff meetings begin to tail off and the sales drive is over.

On this morning, the young people who were coming to pick up Jamie experienced a flat tire and stopped in front of a local motel. As they waited for help, they couldn't help but notice a familiar figure coming out of one of the rooms of the motel with a stranger. It was Valerie, Jamie's mom. They then got into the Uber vehicle, gave each other a long kiss and drove off.

Jamie's friends were in shock and didn't quite know how to share the news with Jamie when they finally arrived at her home. Before they got to the school, one of the girls finally told her that she saw her mother kissing the Uber driver. When Jamie saw her mother later that evening, she confronted her mother who first said that it was not her, but later admitted that it was.

Valerie would later call one of Victor's friends to the house to be there when she told him that she had been having an affair with the Uber driver. Victor had to be restrained by his friend while Valerie gave the unpleasant details of what would be the ultimate betrayal in his life.

Valerie was asked to go live with her mother while Victor and Jamie processed one of the worst days of their lives. At this point, he knows that his heart has been broken, and that he feels like his world is coming to an end. Valerie's apologetic words seemed to carry little meaning. The more he thought about the affair, the more anger and depression set in.

Valerie, realizing that she made the biggest mistake of her life, would later seek Victor's forgiveness and individual counseling to get some stability back into her life. Victor, in turn, would struggle with both forgiveness and a depth of depression he had never known, not to mention the thought of doing great bodily harm to the Uber driver.

Their marriage reached the brink of divorce until they reached out for professional help and sought divine help to lift them out of a dark place – depression. Some days Victor would feel so sad that he withdrew from conversation about the affair. Other days he would be so angry that he cursed Valerie out demanding an explanation for taking him through this hell. The relationship survived, but not until the depression lifted and Victor was able to see the light of a new day in his love with Valerie and himself. It also helped that they were able to pray together and surround themselves with supportive friends and family.

About 30 percent of those who experience a marital crisis of this type become clinically depressed. Symptoms of depression include the loss of interest and pleasure in life along with several of the following symptoms: irritability, sadness, bouts of crying, as well as changes in appetite, sleep patterns, and activity levels. Problems with concentration are frequently reported, along with feelings of guilt and worthlessness. Decision-making can become impaired. Suicidal ideas or thoughts can arise and are reasons to seek professional help at once. The severity of the depression and its duration must also be considered. If the depression does not begin to lift in two to four weeks, professional consultation is in order.

Have you ever experienced depression? Sir Winston Churchill used to call depression his 'black dog'. Depression is the physical and emotional result of hopelessness – the sense that things are not going to get any better. It's a valley, or a low place of despair.

The answer is to get God's hope back inside of you.

Psalm 23:4 (NIV) *"Even though I walk through the darkest valley, I will fear no evil, for you are with me; your rod and your staff, they comfort me."*

Some relationships end badly, leaving us feeling less than positive. Sometimes there's an aftertaste. Sometimes we're left dazed and bruised. My first serious relationship was my sophomore year in high school. We were very fond of each other, and I had a strong emotional tie to her. Was it love? It sure felt like it. We went places together, talked a lot, and had some romantic moments that convinced me that I was. The sun was always shining. I wanted it to last forever. I was only 15. Forever didn't last long. For about six months this was the best relationship I ever had. But she later began to show interest in someone else. I never knew who it was, but soon found myself without a girlfriend. I never saw it coming. My heart and hopes were dashed. I soon began to feel sad about the girlfriend lost. It was also my first real experience with depression. "How could she do this to me?" I asked myself.

About 3 months later, we were on a surface road headed near her home, talking and walking after some of us concluded playing softball in the neighborhood. We were still friends and always looked out for each other. Before I could react, she looked at me, pushed me gently up against the garage, gave me a simple smile, kissed me on the lips and walked away. I understood. She was saying by her kiss, "There will be others. Love will come again". She was right. My depression soon lifted.

What is depression?

From a clinical perspective, depression often occurs when the brain cannot hold onto serotonin, the feel-good chemical that our bodies naturally produce. Selective serotonin reuptake inhibitors (SSRIs) are drugs that were designed to block this 'leaking' of serotonin from our brains.

From an internal perspective, depression is a turning away from the outside world and closing to everything other than self. I've suffered from depression, and I know how it feels to be so emotionally isolated that nothing seems worth doing anymore. There have been times when I didn't want to eat, sleep, play, or even breathe anymore. I saw myself as a worthless creature, taking up space on a planet where I had become obsolete.

I can recall times when it was difficult getting up, putting on clothes and going to the store; when I really believed that things were never going to improve. Sometimes you have to tell yourself that "this is only temporary. Things will get better".

Depression and anxiety surface when we suppress anger. People who have been emotionally abused usually suffer from depression and anxiety long after they end unhealthy relationships. Many researchers believe that depression and anxiety surface as a result of suppressed anger toward our abusers.

Dr. Paul Meier wrote, "A majority of anxiety disorders involve fear of becoming aware of our unconscious repressed anger toward our abusers or toward ourselves."

Dr. Robert Puff says that depression results from offering quick or false forgiveness to our perpetrators. The result is worse than no forgiveness, because what surfaces is anger. And when we become angry, we feel guilty. To erase our anger and guilt, we engage in unhealthy behaviors aimed at making it all go away, such as: overworking, overeating, drinking, taking drugs, or engaging in other addictive activities.

Why is depression so difficult to overcome?
In many cases of loss or betrayal, we can see that depression is merely a cover-up for suppressed anger and guilt. When we are depressed, we dwell on negative thoughts about ourselves or our perpetrators. In turn, those negative thoughts cause further depression. It becomes a downward spiral which we often feel is uncontrollable.

Dr. Meier asserts that unforgiveness drains our brains of the serotonin that we need to feel happy. He claims that many of his patients have quickly overcome their depression using short-term anti-depressant treatment combined with psychotherapy directed at learning to forgive.

I believe that there must be some truth in this claim, because the depression that has consumed me at times slowly dissipates. It's when I began studying and praying about forgiveness daily that things began to change for me. The closer I came to forgive, the happier I felt.

I would like to say that not all depression is caused by problems with forgiveness. However, I believe that unforgiveness can certainly play a role in preventing us from getting well.

Some scriptures to help you overcome depression:

<u>Deuteronomy 31:8</u> (NIV)
"The Lord himself goes before you and will be with you; he will never leave you nor forsake you. Do not be afraid; do not be discouraged."

Psalm 27:14 ^(NIV)

"Wait on the LORD: be of good courage, and He shall strengthen thine heart: wait, I say, on the LORD."

Psalm 34:18, 19 ^(NIV)

"The LORD is close to the brokenhearted and saves those who are crushed in spirit. ¹⁹A righteous man may have many troubles, but the Lord delivers him from them all."

Psalm 43:5 ^(NIV)

"Why are you downcast, O my soul? Why so disturbed within me? Put your hope in God."

Philippians 4:6-7 ^(NIV)

"Be anxious for nothing, but in everything by prayer and supplication with thanksgiving let your requests be made known to God. And the peace of God, which surpasses all comprehension, will guard your hearts and your minds in Christ Jesus."

When you forgive and still hold a grudge...is like driving forward with your foot on the brake.

January 4, 2010 by Anonymous in Forgiveness
ID#:259331

CHAPTER 6

THE TRAUMA OF BETRAYAL

When you experience a traumatic event, it is deeply disturbing to you emotionally. The worst betrayal that I have ever experienced has been by people that I have shared ministry with. This is not an indictment against the church, but rather a sobering truth that people who function in the name of the Lord are also capable of acting in ways that can cause deep wounds to your soul.

This person, who was a friend for no less than 25 years, out of the blue, decided to end our relationship through an email. This was followed by conversations and untruths told to others as to why the relationship ended, but with no effort to communicate verbally with me. It's amazing how people will swear that they tried to contact you, but that the email was the only way. But I have learned that when people really want something, they have no trouble making personal contact with you.

This kind of trauma is associated with sadness, anger, and loss. It's not healthy to take this kind of betrayal by waving it off as though it didn't matter. It did matter, and it did hurt. If I didn't confront it or act, then depression would have set in and taken me into a valley of sadness or low self-confidence. I couldn't allow that. So, I chose to confront the person, although the wrongs were not acknowledged.

You see an enemy can be removed from your immediate thoughts and concerns and does not have to matter to you. When it's an inside job, it affects you differently. To talk about it was cathartic for me.

When a trust is violated, it's like someone who has the key to your house, who enters when you are not there, take your valuables, and leave it ransacked so that you think it was a burglar.

The pain and attacks from former friends are much more severe and tend to last longer. This person may have some suppressed anger that has never been divulged and is prepared to afflict in the worse possible way. Or, the person may have felt slighted and seized the opportunity for reprisal. You see, this person had access to your heart and some of your private thoughts. When a former friend leaves your life, they sometimes feel free to share privileged information with little regard to maintain ministerial integrity or confidentiality. The person who betrays you often intends to inflict as much pain as possible. To do this is to literally say, "I don't care what happens to you".

David experienced betrayal at the hands of Ahithophel in a similar fashion.

Psalm 55:12-14 (NIV)

"12If an enemy were insulting me, I could endure it; if a foe were rising against me, I could hide.

13But it is you, a man like myself, my companion, my close friend,

14with whom I once enjoyed sweet fellowship at the house of God, as we walked about among the worshipers."

Ahithophel was one of David's most trusted advisors. When Absalom, David's son conspired to take over the kingdom, Ahithophel turned his allegiance to Absalom and joined forces with him against King David. This caused him great sorrow as he expressed it in the above psalm. Perhaps Ahithophel harbored some resentment against David and used the conspiracy with Absalom to strike a death blow to David. Fortunately, David had other men like Hushai who stayed loyal to him by remaining in the city and gave better counsel to Absalom to defeat the treacherous words of Ahithophel who really wanted David dead.

2 Samuel 15:31 (KJV)

"And one told David, saying, Ahithophel is among the conspirators with Absalom. And David said, O LORD, I pray thee, turn the counsel of Ahithophel into foolishness."

<u>2 Samuel 17:14</u> (NIV)

"Absalom and all the men of Israel said, "The advice of Hushai the Arkite is better than that of Ahithophel." For the LORD had determined to frustrate the good advice of Ahithophel in order to bring disaster on Absalom."

Because of the faithfulness of Hushai, both Ahithophel and Absalom were defeated, and King David was restored.

One of the keys to David's restoration was that he prayed and asked God to turn Ahithophel's counsel into foolishness. Praying to overturn what your enemy does is a valuable weapon. What we can't do with our hands we can do with our mouth. Renounce it!

Isaiah 54:17 (NIV)

"No weapon forged against you will prevail, and you will refute every tongue that accuses you. This is the heritage of the servants of the LORD, and this is their vindication from me," declares the LORD."

"I Forgave my Husband for Cheating on Me."
Christy Little Jones, 42
Fort Washington, Maryland

"You don't know me, but I am no longer dating your husband...I'm sorry for any pain I caused your family." Christy recalls the exact moment she read that sentence, in an e-mail sent to her last March. "My heart just stopped," says the mother of four (to stepson AJ, 26; and Skye, 9; Blaze, 8; and Hayes, 6). "I felt paralyzed."

Until that point, Christy, a relationship coach, believed that she and Adrian, 46, her husband of 10 years, were happily married. Certainly, things weren't perfect: Business was slow for Adrian, a car salesman, and their bank balance had taken a hit.

"Adrian and I were feeling lots of pressure about money," says Christy. But she had seen no other warning signs. "We still had date nights and did things as a family. I never dreamed he would betray me."

After reading and rereading that e-mail, Christy called her husband at work. Voice shaking, she demanded an explanation. "Adrian was defensive at first, he said it never happened, and even hung up on me," she remembers. "A minute later he called back, crying, admitting it was true, and begged me to forgive him."

The story unfolded: Adrian and a customer had flirted. A one-night stand had turned into a four- month affair. In February 2012, when the woman asked Adrian if he would ever leave his family, he broke off the relationship. "I was furious," says Christy. "It was hard for me not to tell Adrian that we were over and make him hurt as badly as I did." Instead the pair talked and wept together all night.

"Once the initial shock passed, I was faced with a choice," she says. "I could either fight for my marriage or let this event change everything."

I struggled with resentment and the fear that Adrian

would not be committed to making the marriage work. "There were many times I asked him, 'How could you live with yourself? How could you look me in the eye and lie for months?' And to get closure, I needed to know every detail of the affair. It was extremely painful for Adrian to answer my questions, but he did so with humility," she says.

"Forgiving him was the hardest thing I've ever had to do," said Christy, "but his honesty made it easier."

But Adrian also confessed his wrongdoing to two friends of the church. The three of them began meeting each week to pray together to discuss their faith and the importance of integrity in marriage. "I appreciated that he wanted other people to hold him accountable," said Christy.

Christy made a conscious decision to forgive. It didn't happen instantly. For the next six months, she verbally and prayerfully forgave him every day until the pain left.

While on vacation in Virginia last May, Christy and Adrian spontaneously renewed their wedding vows. "We continue to work on trust issues," she admits. "But our marriage is stronger for it. I have no regrets."

By STEPHANIE BOOTH
www.realsimple.com/.../stories-forgiveness

"The disorienting aftereffects of relationship betrayal resembles nothing so much as the symptoms of post-traumatic stress we see in victims' earthquakes and other such natural disasters." Barry A. Bass,
Ph.D.

The only thing worse than an enemy is a former friend.

Bruce S. Riley

CHAPTER 7

THE STREETS OF REVENGE

One of the underlying reasons why it is so hard for some to forgive is the want to seek revenge. The desire for revenge comes from the dark side of betrayal or cruelty from others. Revenge wants to get them back for what they did. It can turn into an obsession and can cause you to lose your focus or objectivity.

When I was a young man of about 17, I began a plot to kill a young man who had humiliated me publicly by pulling my pants down in front of some girls. I wasn't sure if I should stab him or beat him to death with a baseball bat, but I wanted him dead. The consequences of those possible actions never crossed my mind. When you are in the depths of anger for revenge you lose your sense of reason. All I know is I wanted him dead!

Fortunately, I remember my mother giving her soul to the Lord and inviting me to go to a worship service with her. The message I heard turned my heart away from vengeance and caused me to lay aside the hatred that probably saved my life. It made it possible for me to forgive my humiliation and move on.

A woman killed her neighbor's ten-week-old kitten by cooking it in a microwave.

Gina Robins, 31, put the pet inside the oven after a row with its owner Sarah Knutton, and then sent her a text which read: 'The cat? Karma.'

A court heard yesterday that the pair had argued several days before, but Miss Knutton agreed to let Robins use her microwave to heat up a jar of baby food.

She told magistrates she heard a loud 'popping' sound and then a 'horrendous screeching noise' come from her kitchen before finding the horrific consequences.

Robins claimed the kitten must have jumped up on to the worktop while fighting with other cats and managed to shut itself in the microwave. The court dismissed her explanation, calling it 'far-fetched'.

Miss Knutton told magistrates: 'She [Robins] was in the kitchen for a couple of minutes and came into the lounge with the bowl of baby food.

'She was jumpy, really different from when she went to the kitchen. She was fidgety, something was wrong. Then I heard the noise. It was loud like a bag of crisps popping in your hands, then this horrendous screech, a horrific loud screech.'

Miss Knutton, 35, continued: 'I said what the **** was that? Gina said she did not hear anything.'

She said Robins went back into the kitchen and then returned with her hands over her face saying: 'Oh my God, oh my God, I am so sorry, go and have a look yourself.'

Torbay magistrates heard Miss Knutton, a mother of two, was sick when she saw her dead black and white kitten.

She said: 'I was in a state of shock. Gina stared at me. She didn't say anything. She just stared at me.'

The next day Robins sent Miss Knutton a text, which read: 'Remember the saying "what goes around comes around?" It has started already to bite you in the ****. The cat? Karma.'

Robins denied it was a 'revenge' attack after falling out with Miss Knutton, who had called the police about Robins' boyfriend's behavior a few days earlier when he had been shouting outside the house.

She told police: 'I had nothing to do with putting the kitten in the microwave.' But prosecutor Iain O'Donnell, for the RSPCA, said it was 'implausible' the kitten had crawled into the oven and another cat had knocked the door shut, activating the appliance.

Robins, of Torbay, was found guilty of causing unnecessary

suffering and faces jail when she is sentenced next month.

Vet Robert Cameron said the kitten would have suffered. He said its claws were clenched in fear.

Speaking after the verdict, Miss Knutton said the incident had been 'one of the most horrendous experiences of my life'. She added: 'What sort of a person does something so cold and calculating? Evidently someone caught up with the spirit of anger & revenge.

It has been said that holding a grudge is like drinking poison and then waiting for the other person to die. Once you tell yourself to "Let go" of whoever the hurt you, a new freedom will come into your soul. Once you change your focus on life rather than death, new energy will take control of you, and you will be empowered to move on. Once you stop take things out of your hands, then you can see the hand of God operate in ways that you never could.

When you want revenge your heart gets hardened, and you can't feel mercy, you can't feel empathy toward another human being. It's almost like a mob mentality that causes people to operate in ways they would otherwise not act. There's almost something demonic, inhuman that takes over. It what we see happening today with so many road rage incidents.

It was Edward Bulwer- Lytton that said, "Anger ventilated often hurries toward forgiveness; and concealed often hardens into revenge". To ventilate anger is to allow the Lord to see into your soul – to see that there is more to you than how people or unfortunate incidents affect you. But rather, you are purposed to make an impact on the world in such a way that somebody is made better by how they see how you handle a most difficult matter – with courage and calmness.

It was Catherine Ponder that said "When you hold resentment toward another, you are bound to that person or condition by an emotional link that is stronger than steel. Forgiveness is the only way to dissolve that link and get free."

Renee Napier and Phillip and Mary Dickson have lived through a parent's worst nightmare. On May 11, 2002, Napier's daughter, Meagan Napier, and the Dickson's' daughter, Lisa Jo Dickson, were struck and killed instantly by a drunk driver. They were both only 20 years old. The grief was unbearable, but Napier and the Dickson's were determined to help others avoid the grief that they were experiencing. The Dickson's worked through their local Mothers Against Drunk Driving (MADD) organization, and Napier founded The Meagan Napier Foundation with the purpose of promoting safe driving. Napier works to spread her message to as many people as she can in the hopes of saving lives.

The drunk driver, Eric Smallridge, has accompanied Napier to some of her speaking engagements. While still serving his sentence, Smallridge was given permission to travel with Napier to speak and tell his story. He would encourage those in the audience to avoid ending up in his situation. After the presentation, the audience would be given the opportunity to view the mangled car.

Napier really wanted her message of forgiveness to get across. Napier and the Dickson's all lobbied for (and won)

Smallridge's early release, and if that's not a hallmark of incredible forgiveness, we don't know what is.

I encourage you to quickly move past the 'Streets of Revenge.'

"Before you embark on a journey of revenge, dig two graves"

Confucius

CHAPTER 8

WHEN THE HURT FEELS UNBEARABLE

It is important to be reminded that in the course of life people hurt each other. It's a part of the interaction and flow of living. We step on each other's feet. Then at other times it's intentional or out of carelessness. Either way it can have the same effect on us. Sometimes the hurt from betrayal can be unbearable. It can make you want to build up a wall against other people's cruelty. One of the problems of building up walls is that it can isolate you and could keep the right people from getting close to you.

I have come to realize that we are made to share hope and gifts with others who may be trapped in their pain and need permission to release it in acceptable ways. I am so thankful for others being willing to give their testimony on how they've dealt with extremely difficult experiences.

The Bible provides an interesting story of Jabez in addressing ways to handle the difficulties of a painful life. He was born during a most challenging time and needed God's assistance so that he could maneuver with the least amount of harm to himself or others. Perhaps he had seen much destruction, pain, and hurt. He wanted it to stop.

1 Chronicles 4:9-10 (NIV) 9Jabez was more honorable than his brothers. His mother had named him Jabez, saying, "I gave birth to him in pain." 10Jabez cried out to the God of Israel, "Oh that you would bless me and enlarge my territory! Let your hand be with me and keep me from harm so that I will be free from pain." And God granted his request.

The family of Jabez had been devastated. The father of Jabez was not to be found, perhaps dead; his brothers were less honorable – void of a ready relationship with God, no active prayer life, impoverished, fearful, defenseless, defeated, and incapable of being a help to the family. His mother had a normal pregnancy from a physical standpoint because all children bring a measure of pain in the birthing process. This mother was in sorrow, sadness, and discouragement due to the bad reputation and condition of this family. Perhaps the way her husband met his end created for her a sense of hopelessness.

I'm certain that Jabez had experienced his share of his family's calamities. After all, his name means "sorrowful". Consider the emotional load he would have to carry as a sorrowful child; no hope, no joy, and no help. Imagine him trying to fit in with a load of doubt, fear, and defeat throughout his youth. And now, as an adult, full of pain and pity, wanting to pull his family through all this mess and give them a new identity. He wants something different. So Jabez makes a request. Despite his past, he seeks the God of Israel for help. This "man of sorrows" extends his need for change upward.

Four things Jabez prayed for.

1. That God would bless him indeed. – He gets the blessings of God's Forgiveness – the removal of the reproaches of his past.

2. That He would enlarge his coast – He wanted God to expand the influence and real estate of his family's name and portion in God.

3. That God's hand might be with him – to help him, lead him, protect him, strengthen him, and to work a work in him so that all he strives to do, including fighting off the enemy of his soul.

4. That he would keep him from harm and pain – that he would not harm others, himself, and evil ways, and that he would no longer be in pain nor operate through his pain.

God granted that which he requested. You might be in the most unbearable pain, but God wants to hear from you. You may not feel that you deserve it but go for it!

Isaiah 59:1 (NIV)1Surely the arm of the LORD is not too short to save, nor his ear too dull to hear.

"People leave you out in the cold and get mad when you learn how to get warm by yourself."

Unknown

CHAPTER 9

WHEN YOU DON'T WANT TO FORGIVE

What happens should you not want to forgive? It is realistic for you to consider that there are times when your grief and pain can be so extreme that wanting to forgive may be the furthest thing from your mind.

But please consider what the feeling of the hurt is doing to you when you don't forgive.

1. **Not forgiving interferes with the effectiveness of your prayer life.** This means that we hold up the blessings that God would provide us if we only take the time forgive. Take your blessings out of "Lay Away" by forgiving.

<u>Mark 11:25</u> (NIV) *"And when you stand praying, if you hold anything against anyone, forgive them, so that your Father in Heaven may forgive your sins."*

2. **Not forgiving evaporates your joy.**

When you don't forgive your joy dries up and your praise is obviously not as strong. It blinds you from seeing what you must celebrate. What do you have to celebrate? When you forgive, division no longer exists, and you've healed a relationship. Celebrate!

3. Not forgiving weakens your body.

Your ability to fight off disease spiritually and physically is crippled. Your immune system is compromised because there is now a schism between your body, soul, and spirit. Satan may also accuse you before God for holding a grudge. When you forgive you release it into God's hand and healing comes for your body as well as your soul.

4. Not forgiving opens the door for the enemy to work in your life. Satan will accuse you before God when you refuse to forgive. Close that door! Your brothers and sisters are not your enemies, Satan is! Your husband or wife is not your enemy either. Satan would love you to stay disconnected. Don't give him that pleasure.

<u>2 Corinthians 2:10-11</u>^(NIV) *"10Anyone you forgive, I also forgive. And what I have forgiven—if there was anything to forgive—I have forgiven in the sight of Christ for your sake, 11in order that Satan might not outwit us. For we are not unaware of his schemes."*

5. Not forgiving pollutes your soul.

The last thing you need is to have bitterness, anger, and hatred existing in your mind, will, and emotions. It contaminates the purposes and plans of God in your life. If you fail to forgive, the water in your soul will become bitter. Get rid of it!

James 3:11 (NIV) *"Can both fresh water and saltwater flow from the same spring?"*

6. **Not forgiving will torture you.**
When we don't forgive our spirit makes us resistant to God's grace and tortures our conscience.

Matthew 18:33-35 (NIV) *"33Shouldn't you have had mercy on your fellow servant just as I had on you?' 34In anger his master handed him over to the jailers to be tortured, until he should pay back all he owed. 35"This is how my heavenly Father will treat each of you unless you forgive your brother or sister from your heart."*

7. **Not forgiving causes you to entertain thoughts of revenge.** Not forgiving keeps you operating in your own will, which is selfish and wants to act against any hurts or wrongdoing.

Proverbs 24:29 (NIV) *"Do not say, "I'll do to them as they have done to me; I'll pay them back for what they did."*

8. **Not forgiving means you won't be forgiven by God.** That means any sins that you commit will be held against you by God. That can't be good. You hinder God's mercy from being released into your life when you hold

grudges. The unforgiveness of your sins puts your soul in jeopardy.

Matthew 6:15 (NIV) *"But if you do not forgive men their trespasses, neither will your Father forgive your trespasses."*

9. **Not forgiving delays the answers to your prayers.** See Mark 11:25. If you delay forgiving, God must wait before he can answer your prayers. If there is unforgiveness, God wants you to pray that prayer first before you utter any further requests.

10. **Not forgiving means you see the failures of others, but not your own.** Your behavior and spiritual weaknesses should always be the top priority when it comes to dealing with sin. If your life pleases God, compassion will usually follow if you want to help convince your brothers and sisters to change their lives.

Matthew 7:3-5 (NIV) *3 "Why do you look at the speck of sawdust in your brother's eye and pay no attention to the plank in your own eye? 4 How can you say to your brother, 'Let me take the speck out of your eye,' when all the time there is a plank in your own eye? 5 You hypocrite, first take the plank out of your own eye, and then you will see clearly to remove the speck from your brother's eye."*

11. **Not forgiving means you are walking in darkness.** Forgiveness is an act of faith, which is an indication that you are walking in the light of God's truth. Darkness symbolizes evil or ignorance.

<u>1 John 2:11</u> ^(NIV) *"But anyone who hates a brother or sister is in the darkness and walks around in the darkness. They do not know where they are going, because the darkness has blinded them."*

Jesus and the Measure of Forgiveness
<u>Matthew 18:21, 22</u> ^(KJV) *"21 Then came Peter to him, and said, Lord, how oft shall my brother sin against me, and I forgive him? till seven times? 22 Jesus saith unto him, I say not unto thee, Until seven times: but, Until seventy times seven."*

We have the capacity by the Holy Spirit to forgive one person up to 490 times. That is, there is to be no limits to our forgiveness. We are to forgive as many times as we have sinned.

Our capacity to forgive is a direct connection to our spiritual maturity. We must empty out our "I don't want to" Account.

"I forgive you....for everything. But I'm not doing it to make you feel better; I'm doing it to give myself some closure."

January 17, 2011 by capoeirista430 in Forgiveness
ID#:355335

CHAPTER 10

THE SECRETS TO FORGIVENESS

When you are experiencing a severe hurt, rejection, abandonment, or anger, don't be alarmed if it is not resolved immediately…you are grieving. Yes, you can say "I forgive" but this merely begins the process. Just like someone whose love one dies, the effects of that loss will be felt for some time until the final stage of grief is achieved. Some matters that require forgiveness are experienced by the victim like a loss. For example, I had to learn to forgive my father, Matthew, for the loss of a meaningful relationship. I grieved the loss of a father in my life. I was able to forgive him a few years before he died.

My love for my father was automatic, it was never earned. I just gave it. I loved the thought of having a father taking me places, going fishing, making things together, and just spending time together. It was somewhat disturbing at an early age that my mother and father divorced. It was agreed that he would be coming to see me and my other siblings on a regular basis. He would come a few times, bring us a few gifts, and would later come around Christmas. After fourth grade, the visits grew few and far between. I just couldn't understand why he didn't come to see me more (DENIAL). After all, I was a good son who never got into any major trouble.

But then he later married another woman. They had a child who became his total focus. From that point the visits basically stopped. I was very angry that he had another child while never really caring for the ones he had (ANGER). I can recall a time when a neighbor's young chickens somehow got out of his yard and was roaming the alley near our house. I don't know what got over me, but I got a large stick and one by one I chased down those chickens and beat them with that stick until they lay lifeless across that alley. Nobody knew it was me that did it. Perhaps it was the built-up anger. "How dare he have another child", I thought.

I do remember him taking me fishing twice in all my life and spending a few nights with him while he taught me to paint during a summer. I was grateful, and yet felt cheated.

I always felt that I was a visitor into his life and never a permanent part.

Fast-forward to age 22, my wedding day. He came. I was elated that he came. Seeing all of us together gave me a sense of family pride. I was very pleased and expressed my gratitude for him taking the time to come and meet my bride. It was a great day in my life, and I wanted him to be a part of the next stage of my life as an adult (BARGAINING). Unfortunately, it was the only event of mine that he came to celebrate with me. He never came to any other events.

Matthew Riley's wife seemed dead set at making sure that none of us had any access to him and ruin his life with her. He allowed it. She was mean, rude, and inflexible. She ruled the nest with an iron fist. The last time I saw him was when I drove to Pomona to his home to discuss the many years that I grieved not having an active relationship with him and to clear my feelings. Oddly enough the control his wife had over him was so strong that she forbade me from coming into the house. I would reluctantly meet him in the garage (DEPRESSION). I shared my hurts and pains with him and wondered why we didn't have a closer relationship. He shared a bunch of flimsy excuses about not having the opportunity. I started the process of forgiveness then. I had only seen him once since my wedding. He never met my sons or grandsons.

The turning point in my journey to forgiveness with my father was when I heard this illustration from a trusted friend: If you went to McDonald's and requested a steak, could you get it? "No", the counter person would say. You might ask, "Why not?" "Because we only sell hamburgers here." the counter person would say. If I went to another McDonald's and asked for a real nice steak. Could I get one there? "No" would again be the reply. "But why not?" You might ask. "Because we only sell hamburgers here" would again be the response. Ok, so if I went to the McDonald's in Beverly Hills, surely, I could get a big, juicy steak. Again, the reply would be, "We don't sell steaks here, mostly hamburgers."

Then it dawned on me, I was looking for steak at a McDonald's. My father was a McDonald's. I was looking for him to serve me steak. No matter what my expectation of him was, all I was going to get from him was hamburgers (ACCEPTANCE). So, I stopped looking for steak and began to accept the fact that he will never rise above what he sees for himself. I started to see him as he is and not as I was looking for in him. In my mind I saw myself having a tender moment with him like an embrace…to love him for just who he was.

Secret #1 – Acceptance

Acceptance is a part of the process that we experience, not an end point. In this case, "what will be, will be". I received what he offered and was able to live with it from the perspective of the decision that Matthew made. He decided as to the relationship he wanted. I had to accept his decision, unless at some point in the future, he changes his mind.

After hearing that illustration about McDonald's and hamburgers, the journey continued for a few years more until he died with no formal ceremony. I was never informed that he died but heard about it later from a cousin. I only grieved for who he was as a man, but not as a father. But I did miss him because I came to accept him for what I understood about him without wanting him to be something that he wasn't.

My forgiveness of Matthew was a journey that was deeper than I ever expected. And it happened over many years, not many months or days. Not everyone will or can fully embrace those who have hurt us, as I did, but there is always a struggle that leads us to our own personal and unique acceptance.

Secret #2 – Forgiveness is a Command

Not only is acceptance a key to genuine forgiveness, I want to remind you that forgiveness is a command. It is not an option or a suggestion. Luke 6:37 (NIV) Do not judge, and you will not be judged. Do not condemn, and you will not be condemned. Forgive, and you will be forgiven.

The key word in the New Testament for forgiveness is the Greek word apoluo. Apoluo means "to release" or "to loose" someone.

Earlier in this 6th chapter, we get the context of what Jesus commands:

Luke 6:17-19 (NIV) *"17And he came down with them and stood on a level place, with a great crowd of his disciples and a great multitude of people from all Judea and Jerusalem and the seacoast of Tyre and Sidon, 18who came to hear him and to be healed of their diseases. And those who were troubled with unclean spirits were cured. 19And all the crowd sought to touch him, for power came out from him and healed them all."*

The work that Jesus was doing at this time was to help the people. He is concerned about the welfare of the people. He wanted them healed both physically and emotionally. That's why he would give them his Word. God never gives his word or directives as suggestions. He gives commands. Those who came to be healed were not put into a lottery in which some were healed, and others were not. All of them were healed. When the Lord does a thing, he does it with the intention that those who are in the midst with him receive what he puts out. When the Lord says something that has a promise, he only expects it to be followed to produce the desired result.

It you want the blessing, follow the command "Forgive, and you will be forgiven."

The present tense of the word suggests "keep on forgiving." You want forgiveness to be a part of your character. You must become a forgiver by your spiritual nature. Forgiveness must be an imperative in your relationship with others. It should not be conditional, but a constant in all your interactions. The struggle comes when you try to bargain with yourself and the mercy of God as to whether you are going to follow the command.

The command to forgive is also found here:
Mark 11:25 (ESV) *"And whenever you stand praying, forgive, if you have anything against anyone, so that your Father also who is in heaven may forgive you your trespasses."*

The Holy Bible, English Standard Version. ESV® Text Edition: 2016. Copyright © 2001 by Crossway Bibles, a publishing ministry of Good News Publishers.

When you don't forgive, you change your relationship with God. Consider the times you've come before God, asking him to move on your behalf, pleading for him to do this and do that. Imagine God shaking his head as saying "No, I can't do it". Whether you believe it or not, your relationship with others affects your relationship with God. Remember what the Lord said in **Matthew 18:20** (NIV)

"For where two or three gather in my name, there am I with them."

What he's saying is when you are not together (in agreement) in his name, he's not in it. God is saying that when you pray and there is no unity or reconciliation between you and your brother or sister, "I'm not in it".

Here's another case in point:

Psalm 133:1-3 (NIV) *"How good and pleasant it is when God's people live together in unity! ²It is like precious oil poured on the head, running down on the beard, running down on Aaron's beard, down on the collar of his robe. ³It is as if the dew of Hermon were falling on Mount Zion. For there the LORD bestows his blessing, even life forevermore."*

Ok, here's another point:

2 Chronicles 7:14 (NIV) *"If my people, who are called by my name, will humble themselves and pray and seek my face and turn from their wicked ways, then I will hear from heaven, and I will forgive their sin and will heal their land."*

Could it be that forgiveness is directly linked with the healing of the land (or your body)? What I see here is the importance of having God's forgiveness in your life. So therefore, if you have unforgiveness in your life then God can't forgive your sins. And if your sins are not forgiven, then God won't heal your land or the source of your supply.

Secret #3 – Humble Yourself

The great sin with Israel was to be overconfident and to see themselves better than any other people. They failed to realize that everything that they had become, and everything they received came from God. Their eventual captivity was a result of forgetting the goodness of God and treating people poorly.

See what happened to King Nebuchadnezzar:

Daniel 4:27-31 (NIV) *"27Therefore, Your Majesty, be pleased to accept my advice: Renounce your sins by doing what is right, and your wickedness by being kind to the oppressed. It may be that then your prosperity will continue." 28All this happened to King Nebuchadnezzar. 29Twelve months later, as the king was walking on the roof of the royal palace of Babylon, 30he said, "Is not this the great Babylon I have built as the royal residence, by my mighty power and for the glory of my majesty? 31Even as the words were on his lips, a voice came from heaven, "This is what is decreed for you, King Nebuchadnezzar: Your royal authority has been taken from you."*

He wouldn't change, so God had to intervene to see if he would humble himself. Fortunately, after losing his mind for seven years (which was the mercy of God) he was given a second chance and humbled himself. Too often, pride can be the cause for keeping people from giving God or others the proper credit or to forgive others. Please don't let this happen to you.

Secret #4 – Prayer

Prayer is a vital part of worship. When you come before God you are to yield yourself to his presence, and acknowledge all that he has done, is doing, and seeks to do in your life. Prayer is a time for you to empty your cares and needs to the Lord. By entering his presence, you are to repent and get in step with God. Through prayer you can rest from the labors of your own doing and determine what God wants. Prayer realigns your will and connects you with the will of God.

Secret #5 – Seek God's Face

Seeking God's face is a part of prayer. When you seek God's face you are most anxious to know the will of God. When God tells you what to do in each situation, he expects you to do it. As I said earlier, forgiveness is not an option. The Lord asks you to give account when you come before him. He will let you know if what you have done is right in his eyes. You cannot seek the Lord's face unless you really want him to say, "Well done". That is, you want the Lord to smile upon your actions and for you to know that he is pleased.

If you are really interested in seeking God's face, I challenge you to go before him and ask him what you are to do with that person that you have had a dispute with. This is a time you take things out of your own hands and place it in the hands of God. If you really seek his face, God will tell you the best way, his way, to resolve that dispute. In most cases, there will be a need for an acknowledgement of wrong, an apology, and forgiveness granted. Don't let stubbornness get in the way. There is a good chance God can heal the relationship.

By putting these secrets into action, you will begin to see results in the way you feel about forgiving anyone who offends you.

"Mistakes are always forgivable, if one has the courage to admit them."

Bruce Lee

CHAPTER 11

THE POWER BEHIND FORGIVENESS

The thing that makes forgiveness difficult is a lack of love. I have come to understand that there are some experiences that make forgiveness impossible for us to consider when we are operating from an emotional response only. The heart must allow divine love to oversee any resultant actions. When we can't, or won't love, our spiritual maturity is incomplete. It is simply this: You won't forgive those you don't love.

But what if you hate them? Then love can't work, and you probably won't forgive them. Love is a component of Forgiveness.

But what if you're indifferent towards them? You don't hate them, but you choose not to be close to them. The problem with indifference is that it might not change the hurt or pain that you feel in your heart. Something's got to affect the pain that you feel as a result of treatment from someone else.

You may not agree with me on this, but the people we need to forgive are mostly people we love. When they hurt us, we move the LOVE, and then we allow the other emotions experienced to take its place.

If we are to forgive, we must do something with the LOVE. I believe we must put it in front of the pain, the hurt, the resentment, the bitterness, etc. Then, FORCE THEM OUT by your words, actions, and attitude designed to bring about forgiveness.

1 Peter 3:8 (NIV) *"Finally, all of you, be like-minded, be sympathetic, love one another, be compassionate and humble."*

Wife Donates Kidney, Saves Marriage

After ten years of marriage, Cindy and Chip Altemos were in the long process of getting a divorce. The proverbial baggage they brought from previous marriages seemed too great to overcome, so they separated and even agreed to date other people.

Five years into the painful separation, Chip was in the hospital with kidney failure. With his health deteriorating rapidly, his soon-to-be ex-wife came to his aid—despite Chip's being in another relationship at the time. "He was still my husband. There was no way I could walk around with two kidneys, and he had none," Cindy told the press. "It was the right thing to do." She agreed to donate a kidney, telling Chip there were no strings attached— no written agreement concerning a better share in divorce court.

The transplant took place on February 21, 2007, and a funny thing happened as they both recovered in the hospital: they fell back in love. Chip thought to himself, why would I want to date someone else, when I have a woman who would give part of herself so I can keep living? He put an end to his other relationship and asked Cindy to come back home with him. The two will be married 17 years in October.

Sam McKee, Sunnyvale, California; source: Associated Press, "Kidney Saves Marriage," www.foxnews.com (5-6-07)

It is incredible how some people who have experienced horrific treatment in their lives and yet can somehow find it in their hearts to forgive their offenders. I believe that God builds our love for him by giving us an opportunity to love those whom we have no desire to love.

Luke 6:32-35 (ESV) *"32If you love those who love you, what benefit is that to you? For even sinners love those who love them. 33And if you do good to those who do good to you, what benefit is that to you? For even sinners do the same. 34And if you lend to those from whom you expect to receive, what credit is that to you? Even sinners lend to sinners, to get back the same amount. 35But love your enemies, and do good, and lend, expecting nothing in return, and your reward will be great, and you will be sons of the Most High, for he is kind to the ungrateful and the evil."*

We generally want our enemies punished, but God has some better ideas and goals for them. There was a time when you were a criminal to the kingdom of God, but God never gave up on you. You must never give up on people. It is so important to consider that your life and others really belong to God. He also knows what we need and what we can do. Just believe that God has plans to use you mightily for the kingdom, and there might be a person out there destroying people's lives that He wants you to love and forgive. God has a way of taking a person who deserves death and gets them to become an advocate for the kingdom of God.

Paul, one of the most influential persons in the Bible, was an enemy of God and had many people arrested and killed.

1 Corinthians 15:9 (NIV) *"For I am the least of the apostles and do not even deserve to be called an apostle, because I persecuted the church of God"*

Enjoy this excerpt of "7 Women and the Secret of Their Greatness" and be exhorted to forgive as Corrie Ten Boom did. She was arrested for hiding Dutch Jews from the Nazis, survived the horrors of a concentration camp, and then astonished the world by forgiving her tormentors.

Healing was linked to forgiveness, Corrie wrote.
Each had something to forgive, whether it was a neighbor who had turned him in to the Nazi authorities or a vicious camp guard or a brutal soldier.

In mid-May 1945 the Allies marched into Holland, to the unspeakable joy of the Dutch people. Despite the distractions of her work, Corrie was still restless, and she desperately missed her beloved Betsie. But now she remembered Betsie's words: that they must tell others what they had learned.

Thus, began more than three decades of travel around the world as a "tramp for the Lord," as Corrie described herself. She told people her story, of God's forgiveness of sins, and of the need for people to forgive those who had harmed them.

Corrie herself was put to the test in 1947 while speaking in a Munich church. At the close of the service, a balding man in a gray overcoat stepped forward to greet her. Corrie froze. She knew this man well; he'd been one of the most vicious guards at Ravensbrück, one who had mocked the women prisoners as they showered. "It came back with a rush," she wrote, "the huge room with its harsh overhead lights; the pathetic pile of dresses and shoes in the center of the floor; the shame of walking naked past this man."

And now he was pushing his hand out to shake hers, and saying: "A fine message, Fraulein! How good it is to know that, as you say, all our sins are at the bottom of the sea!"

And I, who had spoken so glibly of forgiveness, fumbled in my pocketbook rather than take that hand. He would not remember me, of course — how could he remember one prisoner among those thousands of women?

But I remembered him and the leather crop swinging from his belt. I was face to face with one of my captors, and my blood seemed to freeze.

"You mentioned Ravensbrück in your talk," he was saying. "I was a guard there... But since that time," he went on, "I have become a Christian. I know that God has forgiven me for the cruel things I did there, but I would like to hear it from your lips as well. Fraulein" — again the hand came out —"will you forgive me?"

And I stood there — I whose sins had again and again to be forgiven — and could not forgive. Betsie had died in that place — could he erase her slow terrible death simply for the asking?

The soldier stood there expectantly, waiting for Corrie to shake his hand. She "wrestled with the most difficult thing I had ever had to do. For I had to do it — I knew that. The message that God forgives has a prior condition: that we forgive those who have injured us."

Standing there before the former S.S. man, Corrie remembered that forgiveness is an act of the will — not an emotion. "Jesus, help me!" she prayed. "I can lift my hand. I can do that much. You supply the feeling."

Corrie thrust out her hand. "And as I did, an incredible thing took place. The current started in my shoulder, raced down my arm, sprang into our joined hands. And then this healing warmth seemed to flood my whole being, bringing tears to my eyes."

"I forgive you, brother!" I cried, "With all my heart." For a long moment we grasped each other's hands, the former guard and the former prisoner. I had never known God's love as intensely as I did then. But even so, I realized it was not my love. I had tried and did not have the power. It was the power of the Holy Spirit."

Excerpted with permission from 7 Women: And the Secret of Their Greatness by Eric Metaxas, copyright Thomas Nelson.
Corrie ten Boom, with Jamie Buckingham, Tramp for the Lord. (London: Hodder & Stoughton, 1975), 217–218.

If we can Love better, I believe that forgiveness won't be so difficult.

The Lord has no desire that we isolate ourselves so we can't be hurt again. Real love will never occur in a relationship if both parties are unwilling to make themselves vulnerable.

When you love someone, you are willing to share your personal thoughts, your feelings, and even your imperfections. In a marital relationship, when a couple makes love for the first time, who gets naked first? I would think it would be the person who is willing to be vulnerable first. They could care less about first impressions, or wonder "Am I the right size? Will I be good in bed? Does my body look right?

It doesn't matter to the man or woman who genuinely loves, because the attention is all on demonstrating love out of a pure and sincere heart. Real love is never self-centered.

"There is no love without forgiveness, and there is no forgiveness without love."
Bryant McGill

Pastor's Bitterness Overcome by God's Love

I heard Paul Yonggi Cho speak a few years back. Yonggi Cho is pastor of the largest church in the world. Several years ago, as his ministry was becoming international, he told God, "I will go anywhere to preach the gospel except Japan." He hated the Japanese with gut-deep loathing because of what Japanese troops had done to the Korean people and to members of Yonggi Cho's own family during WWII. The Japanese were his Ninevites.

Through a combination of a prolonged inner struggle, several direct challenges from others, and finally an urgent and starkly worded invitation, Cho felt called by God to preach in Japan. He went, but he went with bitterness. The first speaking engagement was to a pastor's conference of 1,000 Japanese pastors. Cho stood up to speak, and what came out of his mouth was this: "I hate you. I hate you. I hate you." And then he broke and wept. He was both brimming and desolate with hatred.

At first one, then two, then all 1,000 pastors stood up. One by one they walked up to Yonggi Cho, knelt at his feet and asked forgiveness for what they and their people had done to him and his people. As this went on, God changed Yonggi Cho. The Lord put a single message in his heart and mouth: "I love you. I love you. I love you."

Sometimes God calls us to do what we least want to do in order to reveal our heart to reveal what's really in our heart. How powerful is the blood of Christ? Can it heal hatred between Koreans and Japanese? Can it make a Jew love a Ninevite? Can it make you reconciled to well, you know who?

Mark Buchanan, Your God Is Too Safe (Multnomah, 2001) p. 47; submitted by Darin Reimer, Victoria, British Columbia, Canada

As you have read, the power behind forgiveness is love. Share your love and watch the quality of your life improve.

"To forgive is the highest, most beautiful form of love. In return, you will receive untold peace and happiness."
Robert Muller

CHAPTER 12

FORGIVENESS REQUIRES COMPASSION

To genuinely forgive someone takes something to be present within you that you cannot ignore. Compassion is how you feel in response to the condition or plight of the person before you. When you have compassion, there is a resultant action that follows. It's one thing to feel sorry for someone, and many people do, but they don't do anything about it. Compassion stirs an inner and outer response. Compassion places love before justice.

<u>Matthew 18:23-27</u> (NKJV) *"²³Therefore the kingdom of heaven is like a certain king who wanted to settle accounts with his servants. ²⁴And when he had begun to settle accounts, one was brought to him who owed him ten thousand talents. ²⁵But as he was not*

able to pay, his master commanded that he be sold, with his wife and children and all that he had, and that payment be made. ²⁶The servant therefore fell down before him, saying, 'Master, have patience with me, and I will pay you all.' ²⁷Then the master of that servant was moved with compassion, released him, and forgave him the debt."

It is quite possible that the servant was experiencing some personal pain that caused him to act improperly or neglectfully. There are times that we make poor decisions that get us into trouble. We do make mistakes but thank God for those that can look past our failures and be willing to give us another chance.

Sometimes we can be so "stuck" in our own lives that we fail to feel what others are going through. Remember, the servant asked for some patience. What happened to patience? If you are struggling with forgiving any kind of debt, you ought to ask God's mercy to go with you on this journey. Practicing patience with people that ask for more time will provide you with great grace for your journey.

Sometimes, during your personal loss, you may want to impose the maximum penalty on the wrongdoer. Can you recall those times when you did not receive what you really deserved? That's called mercy. The servant, in this parable, was not only going to have to repay the debt, but he was in jeopardy of losing all his personal possessions, his wife and children.

It was the servant's behavior that generated the compassion in the king. He fell before him, asking for patience, and asked for more time. Sometimes all people need is a little more time. The right behavior will often stir the right response. He was moved with compassion on the servant.

One of the best ways to make things right with someone who owes you is to remove the obligation. To forgive the debt is to take the loss. This is a bookkeeping term. "Father, forgive us our debts, as we forgive our debtors" Write off the debt from the books. You don't really erase it; you write it off the books as a debt paid.

When I saw my father, in that garage, looking whipped by his wife, and not allowed to bring his own son into his home, my heart began to change. Instead of getting angry at his wife, I began to feel a deep sorrow for him. "Is this what Matthew Riley has turned into, I asked myself? In a way, I wanted to get him away from her. I felt some of his pain. After that experience I began to seriously forgive him. I remembered that he could only give me McDonald's.

<u>Colossians 3:12</u> (KJV)

"Therefore, as the elect of God, holy and beloved, clothe yourselves with compassion, kindness, humility, gentleness, and patience."

From that moment, I no longer craved steak (the best relationship possible) from him. I truly forgave him and loved him from where he was and where I was.

You Killed My Son...And I Forgive You

For 10 years now StoryCorps has captured real Americans talking about love and loss, pain and triumph. In honor of their anniversary, we publish this moving conversation between a woman and the man who killed her only son.

MARY JOHNSON, 58, talks with OSHEA ISRAEL, 34

In 1993, Oshea Israel, 16, got into an argument with Laramiun Byrd, 20, at a party, and he shot and killed him. Laramiun was Mary Johnson's only son.

Mary Johnson: You took my son Laramiun's life, and I needed to know why. The first time I asked you to meet with me, you said "absolutely not." So, I waited nine months and asked you again—and you said yes. You and I finally met in March 2005 at Stillwater Prison. I wanted to know if you were in the same minds-set of what I remembered from court when you were sixteen. But you were not that sixteen-year-old boy anymore. You were a man. You entered, and we shook hands. I just told you that I didn't know you; you didn't know me. You didn't know my son; my son didn't know you. But we needed to get to know one another. And that's mainly what we did for two hours. We talked.

Oshea Israel: I found out that your son's and my life paralleled, and we had been through some of the same things, and somehow, we got crossed. And I took his life—without even knowing him. But when

I met you, he became human to me.

THE JOURNEY TO FORGIVENESS

I still don't know how to take receiving forgiveness from you. How do you forgive someone who has taken your only child's life? To know that I robbed you of that, and for you to forgive me... you can't really put it into words.

When it was time to go, you broke down and started shedding tears. And then you just started going down, and the initial thing I tried to do was just hold you up in my arms. I'm thinking, "I can't let her hit the ground." So, I just hugged you like I would my own mother.

Mary: After you left, I said, "I just hugged the man who murdered my son." And that's when I began to feel this movement in my feet. It moved up my legs and it just moved up my body. When I felt it leave me, I instantly knew that all that anger and hatred and animosity I had in my heart for you for twelve years was over. I had totally forgiven you.

Oshea: Being incarcerated for so long, you tend to get detached from real love from people. Sometimes I still don't know how to take receiving forgiveness from you. How do you forgive someone who has taken your only child's life? To know that I robbed you of that, and for you to forgive me… you can't really put it into words.

I served seventeen years of my twenty-five-year sentence, and since I got out, I see you almost every day. Although I can never replace what was taken from you—I can never fill that void—I can do the best that I can to be right there for you. I didn't want you to wonder what this guy was doing since he got out of prison. And now, you can see what I'm doing – you live right next door.

Mary: It's amazing. We have our conversations on our porch, and we share our stories—

Oshea: They go from "Hey, I found a job opportunity for you" to "Boy, how come you ain't called over here to check on me in a couple days? You ain't even asked me if I need my garbage to go out!" [Laughter.] I find those things funny, and I appreciate it all. I admire you for your being brave enough to offer forgiveness, and for being brave enough to take that step. It motivates me to make sure that I stay on the right path.

Mary: I know it is not an easy thing to talk about, us sitting here, looking at each other right now. So, I admire that you can do this.

Oshea: Regardless of how much you see me stumble out here, you still believe in me. You still have the confidence that I'm going to do the right thing, and you still tell me to keep moving forward, no matter what.

Mary: You know, I didn't see Laramiun graduate, but you're going to college, and I'll be able to see you graduate. I didn't see him get married. But hopefully, one day I'll be able to experience that with you. Our relationship is beyond belief.

Oshea: I agree. I love you, lady.

Mary: I love you too, son.

Recorded in Minneapolis, Minnesota, on April 18, 2011. www.rd.com/.../inspiring-forgiveness-stories

> "If you do not forgive, you're just the same as the person who did the mistake in the first place."
> Your average eccentric orange

CHAPTER 13

THE GIFT OF FORGIVENESS

The Gift of Forgiveness is extending a quality of yourself willingly, without expecting the gift to be repaid by the one it is extended to. After all, it is a gift. You choose to give a gift as an expression of love or thanks. When I think of any gifts I've given in the past, it's given with the attitude of "I'm so blessed, I can afford to release you from any debt."

The Prodigal son's father is a prime example of someone giving the Gift of Forgiveness.

<u>Luke 15:11-32</u> (ESV) *"¹¹And he said, "There was a man who had two sons. ¹²And the younger of them said to his father, 'Father, give me the share of property that is coming to me.' And he divided his property between them. ¹³Not many days later, the younger son gathered all he had and took a journey into a far country, and there he squandered his property in reckless living.*

¹⁴And when he had spent everything, a severe famine arose in that country, and he began to be in need. ¹⁵So he went and hired himself out to one of the citizens of that country, who sent him into his fields to feed pigs. ¹⁶And he was longing to be fed with the pods that the pigs ate, and no one gave him anything.

¹⁷"But when he came to himself, he said, 'How many of my father's hired servants have more than enough bread, but I perish here with hunger! ¹⁸I will arise and go to my father, and I will say to him, "Father, I have sinned against heaven and before you. ¹⁹I am no longer worthy to be called your son. Treat me as one of your hired servants."' ²⁰And he arose and came to his father. But while he was still a long way off, his father saw him and felt compassion, and ran and embraced him and kissed him. ²¹And the son said to him,

'Father, I have sinned against heaven and before you. I am no longer worthy to be called your son.²²But the father said to his servants, 'Bring quickly the best robe, and put it on him, and put a ring on his hand, and shoes on his feet. ²³And bring the fattened calf and kill it, and let us eat and celebrate.

²⁴For this my son was dead, and is alive again; he was lost, and is found.' And they began to celebrate."

Here's what we learn from the Prodigal Son's Father:
1. **Never ask that someone stay.** You can't make someone stay who wants to leave your life. Give people kindness, even if you believe they are making the biggest mistake of their lives.

2. **Believe that you have done what you were supposed to**. He had a well-run household and was preparing his two sons to run the family business. Too often we experience people that are impatient and choose not to follow the prescribed system. You should be on alert when there are those who don't have the Father's Vision. Keep focused on the job at hand. It will pay great dividends later.

3. **Don't chase after someone who has left**. The father had many resources whereby he could have put on a search and gone after his son. He probably had an inkling that his son was not yet prepared to face the world at this stage of his life. His wisdom told him that if he went after his son he would only leave again. He didn't want that to happen. It had to be by his choice. It broke his heart to have his son leave; it probably hurt worse if others brought him news of what was happening to his son. He had to come back on his own. The scriptures don't say how long he was gone, but we know that Israel had been alienated from God for a considerable amount of time. After all, this parable is about repentance and restoration.

4. **Prayer and repentance precedes forgiveness**. The father, no doubt, prayed that God forgive him for any errors or mistakes that he made as a father, and sought an opportunity to make things right. He prayed that his son would come to himself; that he realizes that he was impulsive and seeks a way back home.

5. **Prepare your heart to receive people back.** Having prayed, repented, and come to terms with his own

issues & flaws, the father put himself into the shoes of his son. What would he be thinking? What if things don't work out? What if he wants to come back home? How do I feel about him now? If someone has left your life, these are some of the questions that come to your mind. The father had to answer those questions in advance…and wait.

6. **Show the Forgiving behavior.** The son decided that it was time for him to come home after having wasted all the money on women, alcohol, and wild parties. And now, having shamed himself, hungry and hurting, he heads back. The father, having already prepared for his return, could have chosen to make him gravel back; he could have ignored him and take him in as a servant. But instead, he saw him coming. In his heart, he saw him coming. In his prayers, he saw him coming. He was not surprised but was expecting his return.

His next act of forgiveness (besides forgiving him in prayer) was to show it by going out to greet him. Please don't let pride stop you from showing your joy when that person you've longed for shows up. Then he gave him gifts. He didn't deserve them, but the father gave him gifts. This demonstrated the value that he placed on this relationship. Real forgiveness places value on the person so much so that it overwhelms them. While the Prodigal son was content on being a servant, his father chose to elevate him, or at least demonstrate to him what he saw his potential to be…ROYALTY. When you and I show real forgiveness, we project faith, or give gifts of life and love to those you have been impressed upon by God to honor. Real forgiveness should have an impact in someone's life.

Comma Moved

Alexander III was Tsar of Russia from 1881-1894. His rule was marked by repression, and by persecution of Jews. His wife, Maria Fedorovna, provided a stark contrast, being known for her generosity to those in need. On one occasion her husband had signed an order consigning a prisoner to life in exile. It read simply "Pardon impossible, to be sent to Siberia." Maria changed that prisoner's life by moving the comma in her husband's order. She altered it to "Pardon, impossible to be sent to Siberia."

In Christ God has changed the comma that stood against us. From "Pardon impossible, send to Siberia" comes the good news of salvation: "Pardon, impossible to send to Siberia."

Sources: biography.com and Today in the Word, July 14, 1993.
storiesforpreaching.com/.../forgiveness

'Forgiveness changes the future not the past'

August 8, 2012 by evathought in Forgiveness
ID#:522996

CHAPTER 14

THE APOLOGETIC FORGIVER

People who know about the place of forgiveness have also developed the capacity to say, "I'm Sorry", or to apologize. It is very difficult, if not impossible, to develop the capacity to grant forgiveness to someone, who you hope will one day apologize, unless you have gained the grace from God to apologize to others for the flaws in your character that occasionally flare up.

We were preparing our sons for school one morning, and things were going fine. The boys, Dorian and Jason, both in elementary schools, had just eaten breakfast, and were gathering their books and other supplies. Everything appeared to be in order and the boys had been doing well on their schoolwork. My wife, Karen was preparing to go to work, and I was getting ready to go to the church.

Now, at that time of my life, I was probably a tyrant of a father, and not that easy to get along with. Jason was dragging that morning, and not focused on what I asked him to do. I was getting upset. When I gave another directive to hurry up, Jason mumbled something under his breath and turned his back on me. Suddenly, I kicked him in his behind and told him to "hurry up." Even as I think about that incident, shame comes across my soul. He seemed a bit shaken, frowned, and just hurried along so I could get them to school on time.

Later that morning, it was like I had a visitation from God concerning my behavior. The Spirit of God overtook me and brought a conviction on me unlike anything I've ever felt. He let me know that I had sinned against Him and my son for kicking him. I couldn't do anything else that morning but repent for having attacked my son. I have never felt that bad in my life. I had to stop immediately (I was doing some administrative work) and go to his school. Nothing else was more important. I got permission to go to his class and asked if I could speak to him. These are the words I used. "Jason, I was very wrong for kicking you this morning. I promise never to do that again. Will you forgive me?" He said "yes". We hugged, and he went back into his classroom. I think he was in the fourth grade.

Jason and I were talking on the phone not too long ago about his son, Justice. I told him about the kicking incident just to let him know that I made a lot of mistakes as a parent. He said, "I don't remember that" "Wow", I said to myself. It seems that the power of forgiveness is really that strong. It made me remember how God treats our sins.

Micah 7:18-19 (NKJV)

"18Who is a God like you, who pardons sin and forgives the transgression of the remnant of his

inheritance? You do not stay angry forever but delight to show mercy. [19] You will again have compassion on us; you will tread our sins underfoot and hurl all our iniquities into the depths of the sea."

That incident taught me a valuable lesson about impulse control and the greatness of my sons forgiving love.

Psychologist Andrew Howell and his colleagues at Grant MacEwan University in Edmonton conducted a study examining the personalities of people more likely to apologize.

From the beginning, Howell was confident that people with high marks for compassion and agreeability would be willing apologizers—and the study results confirmed his hypothesis.

By Lauren F. Friedman on November 1, 2011

People like me, who are compassionate and agreeable generally, are very sensitive to the feelings and conditions of other people. Many times, I apologize for the things that would affect me if I were on the other side of my words. I don't want my words to wound or grieve others.

Here's what I've learned so far about an apology:

• An apology helps bring healing to a relationship, especially when you see how you may have contributed to the problem.

• An apology is a way to restate what you meant to say when your words may have been spoken with anger or bitterness.

• An apology opens the door for reconciliation when a standoff has occurred.

• An apology is taking responsibility for maintaining

93

communication when two people stop talking.

• An apology is recognizing that you may have been trying to prove yourself right when really you want to come together to do what is right.

• An apology is acknowledging to others when you may have been harboring any bitterness or resentment.

• An apology is admitting withholding information that could have been useful in helping someone avoid making a bad decision.

• An apology should come from a place of regret. It should bother you not to apologize.

Please keep in mind, some people never apologize, but there are some that will apologize and are in torment until they do.

But also bear in mind there are those who need to forgive others and are also in torment and really need to be forgiven.

Here's what I've learned so far about forgiveness:
• Forgiveness does not always require an apology, but it makes it easier for one.

<u>Luke 23:34</u> (NIV) *Jesus said, "Father, forgive them, for they do not know what they are doing."*

• Forgiveness is an act of the will. It is a choice.
• Forgiveness will change your life.
• Real forgiveness releases & extends love.
• Forgiveness affects your behavior.
• Forgiveness can end one's grief.
• Forgiveness is a gift that can save a life.
• Forgiveness is divine. It comes from the heart of God

People who have come to exercise the power of forgiveness have done so by learning how to apologize (repent) for their own sins, and therefore make it easier for them to forgive others.

1 John 1:9 (NIV) *" If we confess our sins, he is faithful and just and will forgive us our sins and purify us from all unrighteousness."*

Matthew 6:15 (NIV) *"But if you do not forgive others their sins, your Father will not forgive your sins."*

A Mother Forgives

In June 1973, Marietta Jaeger went camping in Badlands National Park with her husband, Bill, and their five children. As they slept in their tents one night, their seven-year-old daughter, Susie, was kidnapped. Marietta suffered all the pain and emotional turmoil you would expect in such a nightmarish situation. In the days immediately following the abduction, she was surrounded by people who talked about the kidnapper in venomous terms, routinely characterizing him as inhuman (even though his identity and gender were still a mystery). Despite this climate of anger and vengeance, something inside Marietta began to shift as the days of waiting turned into weeks. As reported in the May/June 1998 issue of Health Magazine, Marietta heard a voice. "What Marietta heard was God telling her, 'I don't want you to feel this way.' As she pondered the message, the weight on her chest seemed to lift and her stomach relaxed.

She fell into the first deep sleep since Susie vanished." This was the beginning of her commitment to releasing her anger and finding a path to forgiveness.

One year after the abduction the kidnapper called Marietta's home. Because she had used the intervening months praying for forgiveness – searching within for the strength to find the humanity buried somewhere within the kidnapper – she was able to convey genuine empathy as she spoke with him. Despite the obvious risks to the kidnapper, Marietta kept him on the phone for more than an hour, ultimately providing the FBI with enough information to locate and capture him. His name was David Meirhofer. He had abducted and killed other children. In FBI custody, he confessed to murdering Susie Jaeger a week after taking her from the family's tent. A few hours later, he committed suicide.

Given Meirhofer's horrific revelation, it would be understandable for Marietta to abandon the course of forgiveness. Her husband never let go of his anger and he died of a heart attack at 56 after suffering for years with bleeding ulcers, but Marietta stayed the course. She began travelling around the country to speak with others about forgiveness, sharing her experience. She even befriended the kidnapper's mother, Eleanor Huckert. "She and Huckert went together to visit the graves of their children," the Health article concludes. "Afterward, the two mothers sat at the Huckerts' dining room table sipping coffee and thumbing through old scrapbooks. There was David on the front porch – a rosy-cheeked little boy, scrubbed and eager to set out for his first day of school. As she studied the smiling boy in the snapshot, Marietta felt that her struggle to invest the faceless criminal with humanity was complete. 'If you remain vindictive, you give the offender another victim,' she says. 'Anger, hatred, and resentment would have taken my life as surely as Susie's life was taken.'"

Source: reported by The Forgiveness Project
storiesforpreaching.com/.../forgiveness

"Apologizing does not always mean that you are wrong, and the other person is right. It just means that you value your relationship more than your ego."
-Unknown

CHAPTER 15

TURNING THE CORNER

FORGIVENESS FOR SELF

"Father, today I ask forgiveness for all the negative and harmful words I have spoken about others. I also ask your forgiveness for hurtful behavior that I have displayed in ways that have caused pain to others. Have mercy on me and tread my sins underfoot and hurl all my iniquities into the depths of the sea. In the name of Jesus, Amen."

PRAYER FOR FORGIVENESS FOLLOWING AN AFFAIR.

"Father, I had an affair and I feel terrible. I really messed up. I have sinned against you and my spouse. I acted out of my lust and knew that it was wrong. I broke it off and desire that you will help me save my marriage. Lord, I am so sorry, and I ask that you forgive me for my sin. I pray that you will help my spouse heal and ultimately forgive me when I confess this sin. I deeply regret my bad decision and pray you bring me closer to yourself through this. In the name of Jesus, Amen."

FORGIVENESS FOR OTHERS (1)

"Father, today with your help I renounce & remove from my life, all bitterness, rage, anger, harsh words, and slander, as well as all types of evil behavior. Instead, I choose to forgive, show kindness, and be tenderhearted to _____ and others who have hurt me, just as you have forgiven me." (Ephesians 4:31-32, (NLT))

"Thank you for your gift of forgiveness.
Help me release the hurt and begin to love as you love. Let me see the one who hurt me through your eyes, in Jesus' name, Amen"

"Father, help me set free and release them to You [Romans 12:19]. Help me heal and bless those who have hurt me [Romans 12:14]. I choose to be kind and compassionate, forgiving others, just as You forgave me [Ephesians 4:32]. Father, "let your peace rule in my heart." (Col. 3:15)

With your gratitude and love, I can draw closer to you and let go of unforgiveness. With your forgiveness, I can see the person who caused my pain as a child of the Most High God. In the name of Jesus, Amen."

(3)

"Dear God, please help me to forgive _____ for hurting my feelings. Help me to see the greatness in [him/her] and to love [him/her] the way that You do. Help me to relinquish the anger that I'm experiencing so that I can walk in the fruit of love, joy, peace, patience, kindness, goodness, faithfulness, gentleness and self-control. Help me to heal from this incident and to release any bitterness that I may be harboring. Please give me wisdom, guidance, and love in this situation so that I can approach it in the way that is most pleasing to You. In the name of Jesus, Amen"

To Forgive Husband's affair

"Father, help me forgive my husband for the affair he has had. Please help me to believe his words (that this will never happen again). Please guide my eyes and heart to see the good and positive changes he is doing to improve our relationship. But also help my husband to learn to speak with honesty, sincerity, and empathy. Father help my husband to be the best man he can be, to forgive himself, and to see his real value. And Father, help me to realize that I cannot change the past, but can work with my husband on building a better marriage today for a better future. Thank you for forgiveness, in the name of Jesus, Amen."

To Forgive Wife's affair

"Father help me forgive my wife for the affair she has had. Please help me believe her words (that this will never happen again). Please guide my eyes and heart to see the good and positive things she is doing to improve our relationship. Show me how to love her the way she needs to be loved, and not to hold this over her head. Father help my wife to be the best woman she can be, to forgive herself, and to see her real value. And Father, help me realize that I cannot change the past, but can work with my wife on building a better marriage today for a better future. Thank you for forgiveness, in the name of Jesus, Amen."

A Forgiveness Prayer to Apologize

"Father, I treated _____ wrong. I know I need to apologize. I have no excuse for my bad behavior. I had no good reason for harming them. I pray that you place forgiveness on their heart. Mostly, though, I pray that you give them peace for when I do apologize. I pray that I can make the situation right for them and that I don't give them the impression that this is normal behavior for people who love you, Lord. I know you ask that our behavior be a light unto others, and my behavior certainly was not. Lord, I ask that you give us both the strength to get through this situation and come out the other side better and more in love with you than before. In the name of Jesus, Amen."

When You Need to Forgive Someone Who Hurt You

"Lord, I am angry. I am hurt. _____ hurt me. I feel so betrayed, and I know you say that I should forgive them, but I don't know how. I just don't know how to get over these emotions. Lord, I ask that you give me the strength to forgive. I ask that you place on my heart a spirit of forgiveness. I know this person said they were sorry. They know what they did was wrong. I may never forget what they did, and I'm sure our relationship will never be the same, but I don't want to live with this burden of anger and hatred any longer. Lord, I want to forgive. Please, Lord, help my heart and mind embrace it. In the name of Jesus, Amen."

"Forgiveness is not something we do for other people. We do it for ourselves to get well and MOVE ON."

-Unknown

CHAPTER 16

DROP IT

You have been forgiven so much. Telling others how much you have been forgiven should be something you should obligate yourself to do. You and I have no time for being critical or condemning. Being judgmental of others is an indication of ingratitude and seems to invalidate the kindness and mercy that Jesus has shown to us.

<u>John 8:1-11</u> (NIV) *¹ Jesus returned to the Mount of Olives, ² but early the next morning he was back again at the temple. A crowd soon gathered, and he sat down and taught them. ³As he was speaking, the teachers of religious law and the Pharisees brought a woman who had been caught in the act of adultery. They put her in front of the crowd.*

⁴"Teacher," they said to Jesus, "this woman was caught in the act of adultery. ⁵The Law of Moses says to stone her. What do you say?"

⁶They were trying to trap him into saying something

they could use against him, but Jesus stooped down and wrote in the dust with his finger. ⁷They kept demanding an answer, so he stood up again and said, "All right, but let the one who has never sinned throw the first stone!" ⁸Then he stooped down again and wrote in the dust.

⁹When the accusers heard this, they slipped away one by one, beginning with the oldest, until only Jesus was left in the middle of the crowd with the woman. ¹⁰Then Jesus stood up again and said to the woman, "Where are your accusers? Didn't even one of them condemn you?"

¹¹"No, Lord," she said.

And Jesus said, "Neither do I. Go and sin no more."

People sin every day. You do too? Some of it might not be identifiable by behavior, but it's still sin if the mind ventures into areas that the body would welcome participating. Too often, some are weak to the point that the flesh accommodates the lust of the flesh. It's good to know that Jesus is always nearby should we find ourselves in a bind.

Jesus was more concerned with relationships than with the inflexibility of the law, which the Jewish leaders often fought him on. Thus, the woman who was caught in the act of adultery was being used as a pawn to catch Jesus compromising the law. The people had already gathered their stones and readied themselves to execute sentence on one half of the perpetrators (I guess the men started getting a pass very early in history). But instead of responding to their question about the Law of Moses and the stoning of a woman who commits adultery, Jesus got them to reset their focus. He would get them to look at themselves. They were waiting on his Word. Before we make any hasty moves or decisions, it is always wise to wait for his Word.

The religious leaders were waiting to know what Jesus had to say about this woman who they already considered guilty. They were anxious to shed blood. They considered her worse than the man she was committing adultery with. But was she? I wonder if they knew her story if they would feel differently about this woman; somebody's daughter, perhaps somebody's mother. Women for years have been degraded by the men who seek sexual favors at their expense. Men can justify their wretched behavior with women they call Ho's (whores) or worse. The rationale behind such dehumanizing behavior will allow them to treat them with less sympathy or pity. After all, she's just a Ho. It's ok to pass her along to other men because she is just a Ho. The man is probably an upstanding citizen, but not this Ho; this vile creature, who doesn't deserve to be treated with respect. I wonder how many of the men with stones had slept with this instrument of lust. Should not the stones be directed towards them?

So, Jesus waited, and wrote on the ground. No, I don't know what Jesus wrote on the ground. Some say that perhaps Jesus wrote their sins or the names of those who slept with this woman. It preaches well, but I don't know. He knew the power of silence and built up to the climactic moment that would change everything. The crowd grew restless, ready to throw their stones, and demanded an answer. But they weren't ready for this answer.

When Jesus rose up, he says, "...let the one who has never sinned throw the first stone!" Each of them, with the desire for justice, and being reminded of their own failures, realizes that the mercy of God has been applied to their sin. She is bound to die, and they are free. This can't be right. They thought that they were interrupting the teachings of Jesus to have a stoning. Instead, Jesus continues the lesson by showing them that compassion always comes before condemnation.

They all dropped their stones and began to walk away, beginning with the oldest. Why the oldest first? No doubt, because of his age, he had committed the more sins than all of them. Forgiveness is an act of dropping your stones, or the remembrance of the mercy of God on your own life to the extent that you 'let it go'. They were all so adamant that this woman deserves to die for what she had done. Now they are reminded that they all should have died for what they had done. How quickly we forget.

Now Jesus issues a declaration of divine forgiveness. He asks, "Where are your accusers. Isn't there one left to condemn you?" She replies, "No Lord" Jesus dismisses the trial and execution – "Neither do I condemn you, so go and sin no more". He is forgiving what she did to others, and to God. He drops it.

The message in all this is to release or drop the case you have against others for what they have done to you. You may be right, but what personal damage have you done to yourself for holding on to all the details of what was done wrong to you. You might get your justice but at what cost? You can lose sleep; lose friends, money, and peace of mind, your health, or even the wisdom of God by holding that person responsible for your wellbeing. You should drop it.

The very thing that you may be holding onto can so weigh you down that you become incapable of having a peaceful and joyful life. Is that situation running through your mind right now? Are you angry just thinking about what that person said or did to you? Do you envision God pouring out his wrath upon them for mistreating you in such a cruel way? If your mind is full of the hurts and betrayal of others, you could be missing out on the opportunities to display your worth and value by building up someone who needs you; expressing kindness to the mother who needs food and clothing for her children; or giving support to a friend going through a financial crisis. You become a better person by the people you help. The stones in your hand prevent you from blessing others. If what's in your hand, or your mind does no good, then drop it!

What about Forgive & Forget?

Forgive & Forget is totally not scriptural. You have been made to believe that in order to truly forgive you must never think about the offense ever again. And then you were taught that if you bring the matter up again then you have not really forgiven. I can tell you that this belief is false.

Here's an example: King David sinned many times and yet God forgave David. Did God remember what David did? Yes. How do you know? The Lord recorded what David did in 2 Samuel 11. It is a permanent record in the Bible, yet God forgave David. God dropped it, and therefore David became a man 'after God's heart'.

What about Remember and Surrender?

The things that you are to remember is that God loves you and desires that you prosper and be in health even as your soul prospers (3 John 2), and that you should present your bodies a living and holy sacrifice, acceptable to God, which is your spiritual service of worship. (Romans 12:1)

TEN THINGS WE SHOULD ALWAYS REMEMBER:

1. You Don't Have to Figure Everything Out

It's so easy for us to want to try and figure out all the details of our life. We try and control as much as we can and get so frustrated and scared whenever we lose that control.

Well, God wants you to know that you can stop trying so hard. Learn to let go and hold on to the one who already knows exactly how your life will turn out. When you stop trying so hard to figure things out, especially why you got hurt, you'll discover a peace in your heart knowing that God is with you and will never leave your side.

2. You Are More Precious Than Rubies (Proverbs 31:10)

Don't let anyone make you feel as though you aren't important or that you don't have a purpose in life. God wants you to know in your heart that you are precious, that there is no one like you and that He has great plans for your life.

3. God thinks about you a lot (Psalm 139:17-18)

When you're struggling on how to forgive the one who tried to destroy you, God is thinking about you.

When you're sitting alone, trying to figure things out,

God is thinking about you.

When you experience a huge setback in your life, God is thinking about you.

When you lay down wondering if you're going to wake up the next morning, God is thinking about you.

God is constantly thinking about you and He does this because He really loves and cares about you.

4. **With Faith Truly Anything Is Possible** (Matthew 17:20) God has provided you with the faith to forgive those who trespass against you, as well as the capacity to accept their apologies. The Lord wants you to believe that your heart can heal from the worst of offenses and abuses.

Psalm 147:3 (NIV) *"He heals the brokenhearted and binds up their wounds."*

5. **God Loves You More Than Any Other Person Could** (John 3:16)
Tortured, beat, and hanged on a cross. God showed his immaculate love for you by sending His perfect son to die. I can't think of any greater sacrifice then the one Jesus made for you and me. When you focus on His sacrifice, what He has done for you, you should never doubt how much God truly loves you, and how you should take that love and extend it to others.

6. **Your Good Works Will Not Go Unnoticed** (Hebrews 6:10)

You know, it can be hard sometimes when you put yourself out there to help someone. Maybe you feel as though you don't get any credit or that others don't appreciate just how much time and effort you are putting in to help. For all that hard work, God will one day call you and tell you, "My child, job well done good and faithful servant."

God sees everything, especially when you forgive someone who you didn't originally want to forgive, but instead, you bless them.

Luke 6:37-38 (NIV) *37 "Do not judge, and you will not be judged. Do not condemn, and you will not be condemned. Forgive, and you will be forgiven. 38 Give, and it will be given to you. A good measure, pressed down, shaken together and running over, will be poured into your lap. For with the measure you use, it will be measured to you."*

7. Life Is Not About How Much You Can Make, How Popular You Are, Or Other Material Things (Matthew 6:19-21)

You may never be popular like Beyoncé' or rich like Bill Gates, but you will have something even greater to look forward to and that is the moment when God finally calls you to be in His amazing presence.

What should be treasured is the souls you win to Christ, how you lived before then, and those persons that you were reconciled to through your forgiveness.

8. God Is in Control of Your Life (Proverbs 19:21)

God is in control. You need to really know that no matter what you're going through right now, God has plans to use you for his glory.

Even if you think your life is falling apart, God is still in control! Trust that He knows what is best for you and have faith that His plans are greater than yours and will ultimately prevail.

9. **A Relationship with God Is Really Important** (Matthew 22:37)

If someone looked at your life what would they say is most important to you? Would it be your relationship with God? Or would it be another relationship you have? Maybe your job? Money? Car? House? Education?

Even though some of these things like your relationship with your husband or wife or children are very important, God always wants you to know that a relationship with Him is far more important…by a long shot.

Nobody can take care of you like Him, no one knows you better than the one who created you, and no one knows the intimate details of your life like the one who created your plan and purpose in life.

10. **Loving Others as Yourself Is Also Really Important**
(Philippians 2:1-4)

Let's admit it, people can be difficult to deal with, they can betray you, hurt you in unimaginable ways, and can clash with your beliefs.

It doesn't matter. You are still called to love every single one of them as Jesus Christ loves you.

Jesus Christ clearly set an example of how you should love others and that means loving them just as much as you love yourself.

Forgive others, not because they deserve forgiveness, but because you deserve peace.

Unknown

CHAPTER 17

HEALING THROUGH FORGIVENESS

You have the capacity to provide healing through the power of forgiveness. The efforts and actions you show towards others can make a great impact on how they see God. Hopefully, they will see Him through you. A most powerful way is by showing mercy.

Merriam-Webster defines mercy as:
1. Tolerant behavior of an offender.
2. A blessing that is an act of divine favor.
3. A compassionate treatment of those in distress.

We need to show mercy on our enemies
Proverbs 25:21-22 (NIV) *²¹"If your enemy is hungry, give him food to eat; if he is thirsty, give him water to drink. ²²In doing this, you will heap burning coals on*

his head, and the LORD will reward you. "

What does it mean to heap coals of fire upon someone's head? This term comes from an Asian custom. There would be a fire in the center of town that would be kept burning continually. The purpose of this fire was to allow the people in the village to light the fires in their homes. Each day a young man would go about with a container on his head with hot coals that he would take from the fire and go from house to house. Most mornings would be especially cold, so that by doing this service to others, the young man's head and hands would be warmed as well. This would be his blessing or reward. You teach your enemies how to really forgive and serve others by the way you treat them when they need help.

Joseph's Journey of Forgiveness

In Genesis 37-50 Joseph shows us that forgiveness is letting go of the false belief that somehow you can change the past.

You must believe that you cannot change others, and that you cannot change by yourself. Only God can do this as you let God join you on your journey.

Joseph is just seventeen when he is sold to the Ishmaelites (Midianites) and then to the Egyptians. His only crime was telling his brothers that they would ultimately bow down in front of him. For this wrongdoing, Joseph was no doubt disappointed and hurt by this treatment by his brothers but is not identified as being bitter against them.

[Ask God to forgive you if you harbor resentment or bitterness].

Joseph trusted God throughout his captivity and remembered the dream. Joseph forgave quickly and was rewarded by being placed over the household of Potiphar, an officer of Pharaoh.

[Begin to forgive while you are during the betrayal]

Though Joseph was accused of attempted rape and put in prison (Chapter 39), he never blamed God, but maintained his relationship and prayer life so that his primary gift (Interpretation of dreams) could operate. He was later put in charge of the prisoners. Joseph refused to get angry when his prison time was extended for two years when the chief butler forgot to tell Pharaoh about Joseph's gift (Chapter 40).

[Forgive those people who neglect you]

At age 30, Joseph began to reap the benefits of his forgiveness by being placed over Egypt which helped save lives from starvation (Chapter 41). He is rewarded with a new name from Pharaoh (Zaphnathpaaneah) which means "one who discovers secret things". His gift is now made public. Joseph's gift makes room for him. He is also rewarded with a bride, Asenath. When Manasseh is born Joseph has begun to fully heal from the wounds of his father's house, that is, what his brothers did to him. When Ephraim is born Joseph sees himself prospering in the land of his affliction.

[People who forgive don't always heal immediately]

When Josephs brothers come to Egypt (Chapter 42) seeking corn, he cries, which is proof that he was genuinely forgiving them for selling him into slavery.

[When you forgive, your emotions are prompted by love]

Joseph is 39 when he personally forgives his brothers, although they never really gave a sincere apology for their hatred and envy (only after Jacob died – Chapter 50)

Joseph tells his brethren, after they ask for forgiveness, that they meant it for evil, but God meant it for good, to save many people.

[Joseph then blesses and nourishes them...a true sign of forgiveness.]

When you refuse to focus on your hurts (Joseph) you can shift to your strengths or anointing, which will take you into your destiny.

<u>Colossians 3:13</u> [NIV] *"Bear with each other and forgive one another if any of you has a grievance against someone. Forgive as the LORD forgave you."*

"We are not at peace with others because we are not at peace with ourselves, and we are not at peace with ourselves because we are not at peace with God."
Thomas Merton

CHAPTER 18

PEACE STREET

Going down Peace Street will allow you to develop a different and perhaps better way to discuss sensitive matters by going into it for the purpose of getting peace. It is being in a state of calm or restfulness; it means being free of conflict. Wikipedia defines peace as "being in a state of balance and understanding in yourself and between others, where respect is gained by the acceptance of differences." Forgiveness is not a feeling, but a condition. The condition is Peace.

Romans 12:17-18 (NIV) *17"Do not repay anyone evil for evil. Be careful to do what is right in the eyes of everyone. 18If it is possible, as far as it depends on you, live at peace with everyone."*

It's all about your Approach

I believe that there would not be as many conflicts and the need for forgiveness if people approach each other better. A lot of hurt feelings, angry encounters, and misunderstandings are the result of an inappropriate approach.

Suppose someone that you know well approaches you, and the first thing they say is "We need to talk". What's the first thing you do? Probably the same thing I would do…brace myself for what is about to be said. Why? Because the approach is rather confrontational and is not very diplomatic. Most people would not like to be approached like that.

How you approach a conversation should always follow a very kind and warm greeting. A smile and good eye contact will most definitely make a difference. A calm demeanor will also make you more approachable. When you approach a difficult discussion, see it as an opportunity to solve a problem, not just talk or argue with no intention of concluding. Be optimistic that it can be resolved.

Judy Ringer, the owner of Power & Presence Training, gave some conversation openers that can get good results and promote healthy communications. I used some of these openers during a recent retreat with some couples:

- "I have something I'd like to discuss with you that I think will help us work together more effectively."
- "I'd like to talk about _____ with you, but first I'd like to get your point of view."

- "I need your help with what just happened. Do you have a few minutes to talk?"

- "I need your help with something. Can we talk about it

(soon)? If the person says, 'Sure, let me get back to you,' follow up right away."

• "I think we have different perceptions about _____ I'd like to hear your thoughts on this."

• "I'd like to talk about _____I think we may have different ideas about how to resolve it, but really would love to work on it together so that we are both pleased with the outcome."

• "I'd like to see if we might reach a better understanding about _____ I really want to hear your feelings about this and share my perspective as well.

Below I'm giving you a simple approach to handle most conflicts in a way that allows you to conclude when a conflict develops.

Conflict Resolution in Five Easy Steps.
1. **Approach it**
    • Use tact
    • Use any of the approaches used above
    • Keep a calm demeanor

2. **Share it**
    • State briefly what happened – address the problem
    • How did it make you feel?
    • What did it make you think?
    • What would you like to happen in the future?

3. **Resolve it**
   - Clarify what was said
   - Don't defend
   - Focus on the person and the hurt
   - Apologize – Reverse the behavior and /or the hurt
   - Resolve what to do next time – Is that ok with you? You are making a correction.
   - You should feel remorse or sincerity. The offended person should feel your apology.

4. **Receive it**
   - Accept the apology
   - Restate what was resolved
   - Give up the right to stay mad.

5. **Celebrate it**
   - Thank the person for hearing you
   - Keep the mood positive from this point

EXAMPLE:

Winston is angry because Angelica purchased new living room furniture and twin beds for their two boys without his knowledge. He comes home and sees the furniture. She is in the kitchen preparing the dinner.

W – "Hi Amber. "I'd like to see if we might reach a better understanding about making purchases. I really want to hear your feelings about this and share my perspective as well." (APPROACH IT.)

A – "I knew you were going to say something. You always

have something to say when I make decisions. I didn't say anything when you bought those new shoes."

W – "But I'm really surprised to see new furniture in the house, especially when I don't get paid until the end of the month. This furniture costs at least $2,000.

A – "Actually, it cost $2,500. But I charged it.

W – Angie, please listen to me. I'm a little bit bothered by this. It makes me feel left out of the decision to make a purchase this large. We need to decide these things together. It makes me think that my opinion doesn't matter. Now remember when we discussed our budget last month, and that we were going to use our credit card for just emergencies? (SHARE IT)

A – "But the boys are outgrowing their bunk beds."

W – "I understand that, but we made an agreement that we are going to use cash for all future purchases. It makes me think that you don't trust my leadership for this family. All of this is budgeted for 90 days from now. (SHARE IT) In the future, I would like us to agree together before any major purchases are made, and that we are only going to use our credit card for emergencies.

A – "So what you're saying is I wasn't supposed to get the furniture right now, but later?"

W – "That's right"

A – "And you're saying I can't use the credit card. What

if I need gas?"

W – "We already set aside cash for the gas. Remember, I put it in the cabinet in the can?"

A – "So you're mad?"

W – "I'm not mad, I'm just a little hurt and surprised that you would do these things and not discuss it with me"

A – "You know what? I am sorry for doing these things without involving you. I grew up doing things by myself. I should have never done that. I truly apologize for that, and I will never do that again. You are my husband and I respect you." (RESOLVE IT)

W – "I accept your apology, and I want us to talk about everything that involves our money. And it is our money. I want us to discuss any purchases over $500. We need to make sure we talk about the credit card before it is used." (RECEIVE IT)

W – "I want to thank you for hearing me and allowing me to talk to you about this without us getting into a big argument. Please let me know what might be coming up so we discuss how we can handle it financially." (CELEBRATE IT) Thank you.

A – No, thank you. And I love you! (CELEBRATE IT) END

Because the more than seven billion people on earth are imperfect, personality conflicts are inevitable. How can we make peace under such circumstances?

The Bible offers good advice. It describes the Creator as "the God of peace," whose name is Jehovah. (Hebrews 13:20; Psalm 83:18) God wants his earthly children to enjoy peaceful relations. And in this regard, he takes the lead. When the first human couple sinned against God, breaking off peaceful relations, he immediately took steps toward reconciliation with his human creation. (2 Corinthians 5:19)

Consider two things you can do to make peace with others:
Forgive Freely
What does the Bible say? ***"Continue putting up with one another and forgiving one another freely if anyone has a cause for complaint against another. Even as Jehovah freely forgave you, so do you also."*—** <u>**Colossians 3:13**</u>.

What is the challenge? Perhaps you have a valid "cause for complaint" and feel justified in breaking off relations with the offender. You may also reason that the offender should apologize first. But if the person is unaware of his offense, or believes that you are in the wrong, the conflict will likely remain at an impasse.

What can you do? Heed the Bible's advice by forgiving

the person freely, especially if the problem is minor. Remember, if God kept account of our mistakes, we could never stand before him. (Psalm 130:3) The Bible says that *"Jehovah is merciful and gracious, slow to anger and abundant in loving-kindness. For he himself well knows the formation of us, remembering that we are dust."*—Psalm 103:8, 14.

Talk It Out

What does the Bible say? *"If your brother commits a sin, go lay bare his fault between you and him alone. If he listens to you, you have gained your brother."*—Matthew 18:15.

What is the challenge? Negative emotions such as fear, anger, and embarrassment may prevent you from approaching the person to resolve the problem. You may also be tempted to seek the support of others by telling them about the problem, potentially widening and inflaming the conflict.

What can you do? When a problem is serious and you feel you are unable to overlook it, approach the person to talk it out.

Try handling the matter as follows:

(1) **Promptly:** Do not procrastinate. If you do, the problem may fester. Try applying the advice of Jesus, namely: **"[If] you are bringing your gift to the altar and you there remember that your brother has something against you, leave your gift there in front of the altar, and go away; first make your peace with your brother, and then, when you have come back, offer up your gift."—Matthew 5:23, 24.**

(2) **Privately**: Resist the temptation to gossip with others about the problem. *"Plead your own cause with your fellowman, and do not reveal the confidential talk of another."*—Proverbs 25:9.

(3) **Peacefully**: Resist the tendency to analyze who is right and who is wrong. Your goal is to make peace, not to win the dispute. Try using the word "I" instead of "you." Telling the person "I feel hurt because . . ." may be much more effective than saying: "You hurt me!" The Bible puts it this way: *"Pursue the things making for peace and the things that are up building to one another."*—Romans 14:19.

<u>Matthew 5:9</u> (KJV) *"Blessed are the peacemakers, for they shall be called the children of God."*

Once upon a time two brothers shared adjoining farms. For over 40 years they worked side by side, sharing equipment and helping each other out whenever needed. Then one day a rift developed. It began with a small misunderstanding and it grew into a major difference, and finally it exploded into an exchange of bitter words followed by months of angry silence.

One day the eldest brother, Pete, was out in his fields when a truck pulled up. Out jumped a man who approached Pete

carrying a carpenter's toolbox. "I'm looking for a few days work" he said. "Perhaps you would have a few small jobs I could do for you?"

"Well, yes I do," said Peter. "See that creek down there; it's the border between my brother's farm and mine. My brother keeps it nice and deep to stop me from setting one foot on his beloved farm. Well I'll oblige him. I want you to take that timber over there by the barn and build me a new fence, a real tall one, so I don't have to look over at my stinkin' brother and his farm no more."

The carpenter was glad to have the work, "No worries mate. I understand. Just point me to your post-hole digger and I'll get the job done."

So, the carpenter set about working. Meanwhile farmer Pete drove into town to the cattle auction. When he returned at sunset, he was shocked to see what the carpenter had done. There was no fence. Instead the carpenter had built a bridge and walking across it was Pete's younger brother. He held out his hand and spoke to his brother, "Pete after all I've done to you these past few weeks, I can't believe you'd still reach out to me. You're right. It's time to bury the hatchet."

The two brothers met at the middle of the bridge and embraced. They turned to see the carpenter hoist his toolbox on his shoulder. "No, wait! Stay a few days. I've a lot of other projects for you," said farmer Pete. "I'd love to stay on," the carpenter said, "but I have more bridges to build."

Source: unknown.

"You can accept or reject the way you are treated by other people, but until you heal the wounds of your past, you will continue to bleed. You can bandage the bleeding with food, with alcohol, with drugs, with work, with cigarettes, with sex, but eventually, it will all ooze through and stain your life. You must find the strength to open the wounds, stick your hands inside, pull out the core of the pain that is holding you in your past, the memories, and make peace with them."
Iyanla Vanzant

"You will know that forgiveness has begun when you recall those who hurt you and feel the power to wish them well."
Lewis Smedes

CHAPTER 19

ARRIVING AT FORGIVENESS

Now that you have arrived at forgiveness, you should feel a new freedom, a new feeling of love, and a new attitude towards those former offenders. Look to make better interactions with others. I believe that you have gained healing in your soul and are feeling better in your body since you've been reading this book. I hope that you have been forgiving others through each chapter while going on this journey.

Now that you are here, let's see how much forgiveness has been integrated into your daily life. Place a check mark in the box indicating your response to each statement below.

Forgiveness Assessment

"I Have Fully Forgive Because..."	Yes ✓	No ✓
1. You don't hate them anymore.		
2. You no longer wish the person to totally leave your life.		
3. You don't feel that ache in the pit of your stomach.		
4. You wish this person well.		
5. You still see the scar, but no longer feel the pain.		
6. This person no longer consumes your thoughts.		
7. You could resume the relationship, but with boundaries.		
8. You have compassion for them.		
9. The good memories outweigh the bad.		
10. You still feel the same even when they enter the room.		

"I Have Fully Forgiven Because..."	Yes ✓	No ✓
11. I want my offender to be happy in the future.		
12. I would help my offender if asked.		
13. I stop looking for them to fail.		
14. I see the offence as a point of reference more than a point of pain.		
15. I accept the fact that God loves them like he loves me.		
16. I realize I have done things just as bad as the offender.		
17. I can think positive thoughts about this person.		
18. I have come out of depression caused by this person.		
19. I have repented for holding a grudge.		
20. I no longer avoid being in the same place with this person.		

"I Have Fully Forgiven Because…"	Yes ✔	No ✔
21. I don't mind making eye contact with this person.		
22. I have peace of mind concerning this person.		
23. I am open to a "New Beginning" if there is a reconciliation.		
24. My body does not react when I hear that person's voice.		
25. I am preparing my heart for that person's return.		
26. The desire to love others has increased.		
27. I can sleep well and not have dreams about this person.		
28. I no longer consider hurting this person.		
29. I no longer feel bitter or angry with this person.		
30. I have taken down the walls to keep people away.		

"I Have Fully Forgiven Because…"	Yes ✔	No ✔
31. I am willing to love unconditionally		
32. I am willing to keep them in my prayers.		
33. I no longer feel like a victim.		
34. I feel that God is in control and not the offender.		
35. I can forgive myself for evil intentions on this person.		
36. When I talk about this person it is positive.		
37. I am prepared to forgive seventy times seven.		
38. I have committed this person to God.		
39. I can love my enemies.		
40. I have done some good deeds for those who have harmed me.		

Score your Assessment by placing 5 points next to each "YES" response. Now add your "YES" responses =

Total Score _____

If you scored from 170 – 200 Your Forgiveness score suggests a Great Tendency to forgive.

> **Suggestions:** Continue to be a Peace Maker, make more contacts and encourage others during the week, especially those you have made reconciliation.

If you scored from 140 – 169 Your Forgiveness score suggests a High Tendency to forgive.

> **Suggestions:** Increase your capacity for compassion (Re- read Chapter 12 and do some good deeds for former offenders.

If you scored from 110 – 139 Your Forgiveness score suggests a Moderate Tendency to forgive.

> **Suggestions:** Release more hurts and grudges (Re-read Chapter 17) and seek more positive life experiences by interacting with more people. Do not isolate yourself.

If you scored from 80 – 109 Your Forgiveness score suggests a Low Tendency to forgive.

> **Suggestions:** Increase your daily prayers for the forgiveness (Re read Chapters 11 & 15) and ask God to increase your love for those who offended

you.

Forgiveness is much more than the words we have said. Forgiveness is in the way we live our life and how we treat others. Forgiveness is love. We love others by our actions and not by our words. Once we actually do forgive someone, we'll know what it is to love our neighbor because we realize how our neighbor deserved forgiveness from us just as much as we needed to rid the pain and suffering from our heart and mind. Forgiveness is really the love of Christ in action versus the darkness of sin in the world.

Jesus said to Simon: "Do you see this woman? I came into your house. You did not give me any water for my feet, but she wet my feet with her tears and wiped them with her hair. You did not give me a kiss, but this woman, from the time I entered has not stopped kissing my feet. You did not put oil on my head, but she has poured perfume on my feet. Therefore, I tell you, her many sins have been forgiven
– for she loved much. But he who has been forgiven little loves little." (Luke 7:44-47 NIV)

He Can't Remember
There was a priest in the Philippines who carried the burden of a secret sin he had committed many years before. He had repented but still had no sense of God's forgiveness.

In his church was a woman who claimed to have visions in which she spoke with Christ and him with her. The priest however was skeptical. To test her he said, "The next time you speak with Christ, I want you to ask him what sin your priest committed while he was in Bible College." The woman agreed.

A few days later the priest asked, "Well, did Christ visit you in your dreams?"

"Yes he did", she replied.

"And did you ask him what sin I committed in Bible College?" "Yes"

"Well what did he say?"

"He said, 'I don't remember.'"

Source: reported in Ron Lee Davis A Forgiving God in an Unforgiving World.

> "Forgiveness is an act of the will, and the will can function regardless of the temperature of the heart."
>
> Corrie Ten Boom

CHAPTER 20

YOUR TURN

I've done a lot of talking about forgiveness. I've shown you many examples of people who learned how to forgive some difficult situations. I've even talked about my own struggles with forgiveness (former friends, the woman from the church, and my father) and how it has changed my life. It's now your turn to implement this grace into your life so you can experience God's love in a more profound way.

Can you imagine the strength and faith that it took for Corrie ten Boom, the Dutch watchmaker and Christian who, along with her father and other family members, helped many Jews escape the Nazi Holocaust during World War II by hiding them in her closet? She was imprisoned or her actions. Consider what it took to see many of her loved ones killed at their hands, and then after the war, to even lift her hand to greet and forgive a former S.S. captor. Few of us have stories as horrific as Corrie's, but all of us have personal stories of brokenness, mistreatment, betrayal, heartbreak, or hurt connected to a person or people that we need to forgive. It may feel impossible. If you are still struggling with the rejection, betrayal, or wounds caused by people you never imagined would hurt you, then please know that Christ has already paved the way for you to forgive as well. Forgiveness is for you. Accept it so you can use it.

OUTSTRETCHED ARMS

The sign of forgiveness is outstretched arms. The forgiving father threw his arms around the neck of the prodigal son and kissed him (Luke 15:20).

God has acted FIRST — to save sinful man! His own Son became a man. He then lived a perfect life, in OUR stead. Jesus received the embrace and kiss of Judas and forgave him (Mk 14:45). Finally, Jesus stretched out His arms on the cross and would have embraced us all if we had not nailed His arms to the cross.

<u>**Luke 23:34**</u> (NIV)Jesus said, ***"Father, forgive them, for they do not know what they are doing."*** And they divided up his clothes by casting lots.

He died — for OUR sins. He rose — for OUR justification! Because of the life He lived, then gave in death, God can accept US — rebellious sinners, though we were. "He hath made us ACCEPTED in the Beloved" (Ephesians 1:7). We are counted as righteous in union with Christ (I Corinthians 1:29-31; II Corinthians 5:21).

As has always been the case, man must respond to God's grace. He must believe that Christ is God's Son with a committing, trusting faith. He must repent of his sins -turn the other way in his mind. He must confess that faith before others, by word of mouth and by action. And he must be identified with Christ in water & Spirit baptism, being buried and raised with Him — through faith in the working of God (John 3:5; Acts 2:38; Colossians 2:12; I Peter 3:21).

The same faith that leads to this initial obedience must continue through all of life — still believing, still trusting, and still obeying. Are you "set right" with God? If not, turn to Him this very day in penitent, sincere faith, demonstrated in complete and trusting obedience. Do not reject God's love and grace! His righteous wrath is the only alternative we sinners have. God has already acted to save you. It's your move now.

Right now, imagine yourself embracing each one you need to forgive. By God's grace and in His mercy make the decision to forgive each person for each offense against you. Say audibly: "By God's grace, I decide to forgive (name of person) for (name of sin). Now go and embrace these people.

If this is impossible, call or write them without delay. If they are aware of problems in their relationship with you, apologize to them and ask them to forgive you for not forgiving them.

Then give them a gift (see Luke 15:22). Show the mercy of our forgiving Father. Don't lose any time (Mt 5:25). IT'S YOUR TURN!

Receive the miracle of forgiveness now!

> "Forgiveness is the name of love practiced among people who love poorly. The hard truth is that all people love poorly. We need to forgive and be forgiven every day, every hour increasingly. That is the great work of love among the fellowship of the weak that is the human family."
>
> Henri J.M. Nouwen

THE END

ABOUT THE AUTHOR

The two most relationships to Dr. Bruce Riley are his love for Jesus and his wife Karen. He is the Senior Pastor of Praise Temple in Long Beach, CA. He has also been licensed as a Marriage and Family Therapist for over 20 years. He counsels individuals, couples, youth, and children. As the director of "Solutions with Dr. Bruce", he conducts Couples Retreats, Singles Seminars, and workshops for various emotional, spiritual, and adjustment issues.

Finally, Dr. Bruce loves people, and offers help to those willing to put in some work and obey the Word of God, the foundation to the solutions of all man's problems.

Dr. Bruce Riley, LMFT
License #34085
"A Man of Understanding" Solutionswithdrbruce.com

Other Books written by Dr. Bruce: 'My Lover, My Friend', 'Making Love Work', and 'Simple Keys'.

Made in the USA
Middletown, DE
12 September 2020